BURDEN

BURDEN

COURTNEY HARGRAVE

BLOOMSBURY PUBLISHING
LONDON · OXFORD · NEW YORK · NEW DELHI · SYDNEY

BLOOMSBURY PUBLISHING
Bloomsbury Publishing Plc
50 Bedford Square, London, WC1B 3DP, UK

BLOOMSBURY, BLOOMSBURY PUBLISHING and the Diana logo are
trademarks of Bloomsbury Publishing Plc

First published in 2018 in the United States by Convergent Books, an imprint of the
Crown Publishing Group, a division of Penguin Random House LLC, New York
First published in Great Britain 2018

A catalogue record for this book is available from the British Library

ISBN: HB: 978-1-4088-9261-9; TPB: 978-1-4088-9262-6;
eBook: 978-1-4088-9263-3

2 4 6 8 10 9 7 5 3 1

Text design by Elina Nudelman
Printed and bound in Great Britain by CPI Group (UK) Ltd, Croydon CR0 4YY

To find out more about our authors and books visit
www.bloomsbury.com and sign up for our newsletters

For Beck

If your enemy is hungry, give him bread to eat;
And if he is thirsty, give him water to drink;
For so you will heap coals of fire on his head,
And the LORD will reward you.

—PROVERBS 25:21–22

CONTENTS

FOREWORD

Every once in a while, there comes a story that must be told. *Burden* is one of those stories.

I have vigorously pursued the telling of *Burden* since 1997, joined by producer Robbie Brenner in 2004, and feel more strongly about it at this moment than ever. With today's historic eruptions of racial division and cultural anxiety, this story in its best incarnation has the power to say something crucial about racism and bigotry across the United States and around the world.

I first read about the saga of Michael Burden, Judy Harbeson, Reverend David Kennedy, John Howard, and the Redneck Shop and Ku Klux Klan Museum in the local South Carolina newspaper *The State*. I'll never forget that moment, twenty years ago, when a short write-up about a KKK museum opening in a small southern town became the source of a lifelong pursuit. It was just a blurb, but it penetrated me. Seven months later, another story landed in front of me: "A Tale of Faith, Hope and Hate," in the *Los Angeles Times*. It told of how a Klansman named Michael Burden, the same man who'd opened the KKK museum, left the Klan after falling in love with a single mother who slowly changed his heart, and was befriended by Reverend David Kennedy, an African American minister who led the local protests against Burden's establishment. This story blew my mind. I picked up the phone, called Reverend Kennedy, and asked if I could come to Laurens and see him.

I spent over a month in Laurens, researching and getting to know the people and details of their extraordinary circumstances. For this short but pivotal period, I found myself experiencing firsthand the plight of the American South. I saw a society rife with unemployment, where the old factory towns that thrived in the South throughout the twentieth century had closed their doors and left people without jobs, education, or hope. I got to live among a forgotten sector of society, bearing witness to their struggles and their hatred—but at the same time their love, their tears, and their perseverance. By the end of my time in South Carolina, I knew that this story needed to be told, for it was the story not just of one isolated group of people but of much of America: millions of people divided by history and conflicting points of view, unable to find common ground.

One of the fondest memories from my time in Laurens and the process of making this film was spending time with the members of Reverend Kennedy's congregation, some of whom are featured in this book, and some who aren't. I was struck that people who had so little in the way of material things could have so much love and joy in their lives. I loved spending time at the church and watching all the fun they had. Whether it was the love between Mina Bates and her husband, Henderson, Jan Kennedy concocting "slitch a mo" stew in the kitchen, Too Ray dancing around the front steps, or Toosie (better known as Miss Shake-a-Leg) doing her shake for everyone's entertainment, they all shared one thing: joy.

Through getting to know Mike; Judy; Reverend Kennedy and his wife, Jan; Clarence Simpson; and the whole gang, I learned what it means to find courage in the face of adversity. These people did something truly heroic during the period of time portrayed in this story, all without calling attention to their deeds or asking for reward. They did what they did because it was the right thing to do. Their humility, compassion, and kindness taught me that there is no "evil" in the world, only pain, self-hatred, wounded souls, and disenfranchised humans. I believe this may just hold the key to healing the angry predicament we are in today.

After eighteen years of false starts and unfortunate events that kept *Burden* from getting realized, we finally jumped off the cliff—and without a net. Six weeks before the shooting was supposed to start, we had no funding, no actors cast for Mike and Judy. Only through the sheer faith, tenacity, and unwavering belief of my producer, Robbie Brenner, was this all possible. On the morning after her film *Dallas Buyers Club* was nominated for an Academy Award, Robbie reached back out to me and said, "*Burden* is next." In Hollywood, these kinds of promises are a dime a dozen, but Robbie is not your typical Hollywood producer. She is fierce, incredibly loyal, and cares deeply about creating films that mean something. She willed this project into existence, and I am grateful for her deep support.

Burden is the definition of a "labor of love." I am so incredibly grateful to everyone who participated and gave their heart and soul to the film—especially the actors, who treated the project with so much love and respect. They all traveled to Laurens on their own time to meet with and get to know the real people they were portraying. They treated their representation of those people with the greatest dignity and care, and I was floored by their generosity. Garrett Hedlund, Forest Whitaker, Andrea Riseborough, Tom Wilkinson, Austin Hébert, and Usher—we owe you all a huge debt of gratitude.

In making this movie, I set out to create a very honest portrayal of the people I met in Laurens, revealing some of the darkest strands of our social fabric while also taking care not to vilify anyone. I am so grateful for this book, which expands on the movie and reveals the actual events that took place before, during, and after the period portrayed in the film.

Now, at a time when the world has become so polarized and divided by ethnicity, race, and religion, *Burden* is the true story of one man's struggle to overcome a lifetime of senseless hate against a cultural backdrop of racial tension, economic upheaval, and systemic poverty. A story in which he must face his sworn racial enemy and find a path to tolerance and redemption. It is a story about faith—not simply religious faith or blind faith, but faith in humanity, faith in oneself, and faith in doing what is just and right, appealing deeply to the good within each of us. It is a story that locates the present world's ethnic dilemmas within an individual and the people who rescued his life.

It is all of these things. But at its core, *Burden* is a love story, and it is love that solves all that ails us. Hatred, both along ethnic and religious lines, has cast a dark shadow on our society for far too long, but we can eradicate shadows by shining a light on them. Hopefully *Burden* can become a part of that light.

Thank you for bearing witness to this story.

ANDREW HECKLER
Jackson, Georgia, November 2016

"THIS IS WHAT WE'LL DO"

The city of Laurens sits in the northwest corner of South Carolina in a region known as the Piedmont Plateau, an undulating expanse of verdant foothills and stream-cut valleys, a remote stretch of country that locals call "the Upstate." It's accessible by one of two main roads: Highway 221, which runs north-south out of Spartanburg, passing by, on the outskirts of town, a million-square-foot Walmart distribution center; or Route 76, a two-lane country back road that cuts east-west across acres of pastureland, oak-hickory forests, and pine woodlots. It's small, just a hair over ten square miles, and predominantly residential, such that you could drive right on by without ever having noticed much of a town at all. Nor is there much reason to stop there. But despite its modest size and its rural setting, Laurens has a surprisingly rich heritage, and deep southern roots.

On the west side, dotted every fifty yards or so along Main Street, are some of the more than one hundred properties that, collectively, make up the historic district: Queen Anne and Italianate frame houses set back on wide lots shaded by mature trees, interspersed along the boulevard with Gothic and Romanesque and Victorian churches. The James Dunklin House, a two-story clapboard farmhouse with white columns and blue shutters, built in 1812, operates now as a little country museum. Six lots down is the William Dunlap Simpson House, built in 1839, which resembles an antebellum plantation and was once home to a South Carolina governor.

Nearer the center of town, the buildings are no less historic but more densely concentrated and almost exclusively commercial: two-story redbrick shops packed tightly together like row houses. Names of businesses long since closed are still etched on some of the windows. To stroll beneath the green and blue awnings outside the Midtown Paint Shop or the mom-and-pop hardware store, past the vintage Coca-Cola mural advertising five-cent fountain drinks, feels a bit like traveling back in time. The whole of downtown—a single square block, in the center of which stands the county courthouse—is listed on the National Register of Historic Places.

By the mid-1800s, little more than fifty years after its founding, Laurens had blossomed from a once-lawless frontier settlement into a bustling center of commerce and government. Its courthouse—an imposing, important-looking building done in the Greek Revival style, with grand Corinthian columns and sweeping Palladian staircases—signified the county's rapid accumulation of wealth during the cotton boom. Years before he became president, a young Andrew Johnson ran a tailor shop on the square, where his business would have been surrounded by the offices of medical practitioners and lawmen, wagon shops, gristmills, a confectionary, and nearly one hundred registered whiskey distilleries. Standing on the courthouse lawn—even now, more than 150 years later—it's not all that difficult to imagine the *clop-clop-clop* of horse-drawn carriages or the keening wail of a locomotive whistle.

Laurens experienced a second boom just after the turn of the century, and there are remnants of that period, too. The Capitol Theatre, which opened on a sticky June night in 1926, still occupies a spot on the south side of the square, on Main Street. During the war years—when an average of eighty million Americans visited the cinema each week—the proprietor opened a second movie house on the north side: a narrow brick building with twin second-story balconies, peering like eyes over an art deco marquee, on top of which still stand the old light-up letters spelling out ECHO.

Both theaters eventually shuttered, however, and the storefronts along the square are mostly empty now. FOR SALE signs hang in the windows, faded from the sun. What few businesses remain are mostly consignment shops and payday loan centers.

Continue east along Main Street, and the homes become decidedly less grand: ramshackle Craftsman bungalows with falling-down porches, oceans of trailer parks. Down on Mill Street, snaking up the side of a low hill, is a crumbling brick retaining wall covered in spider-like brown vines; behind it is the hollowed-out shell of Laurens Cotton, once a massive four-story factory, now little more than an abandoned elevator shaft and piles of rubble, streaked rusty brown from decades of rainwater.

Like virtually every other settlement across the Upstate, Laurens is a former mill town, situated in what used to be the heart of the American textile industry. Proximity to the cotton fields and a temperate climate lured the big companies down from the North in the late 1800s, and most of the towns and villages still bear the names of the mills themselves, or their owners: Watts Mills, Fort Mills, Joanna, Ware Shoals. The first squeeze came in the 1970s and '80s, with a flood of cheap imports and the rise of automation. The kill shot came later, in the form of the North American Free Trade Agreement. Laurens County lost nearly all of its remaining mills—and thousands of jobs—in the span of little more than a decade. The smokestacks and water towers are all that's left. Ruins dot the landscape like constellations.

More prosperous towns to the north—Spartanburg, Greenville—have since repositioned themselves as global manufacturing hubs, attracting millions of dollars in foreign direct investment. Laurens, on the other hand, has not fared so well. More than 25 percent of its 9,139 residents live below the poverty line. High unemployment, a flourishing drug trade, and a transient population that sometimes takes up residence in the hollows of the crumbling mill villages have made it one of the more dangerous cities in the state. And for all its quaint, small-town charm, swirling underneath is a darker history.

"I MEAN, I hear them talk about it."

Brock Coggins was born in 1918, five years after it happened, but he grew up listening to the stories. "This colored man raped a white woman. And the lynching took place up there in town. On a railroad trestle."

Rachel Watts heard the stories, too, though she was raised on a farm in an African American community several miles west of town. "When we would go over that trestle, Daddy would say, 'So-and-so was lynched here,'" she recalled in a 1997 interview with historian Bruce Baker. "My father was forever talking to his boys, telling them, you know, 'Don't get yourselves involved in instances where you could get lynched.'"

Samuel Shipman was a student at Ford High, an all-white

school for the children of mill workers, when the *Brown v. Board of Education* ruling came down, and postcard-sized photos of the lynching victim began circulating throughout the community. "They thought [integration] wouldn't happen here," he explained in an April 2000 interview for the Veteran's Oral History Project. "And that picture has been blown up and reproduced so many times of that black gentleman hanging from the railroad truss because he looked at a white woman or something, I don't know the story. But that picture was passed around . . . *This is what we'll do.*"

Just south of Main Street, not three hundred yards from the courthouse square, the sidewalk slopes downhill and gives way to a network of gravel parking lots and dusty side streets, beyond which lies a tangle of tracks. The rail serves only freight trains now; the CSX rolls by every few hours, hauling gas and wind turbines from a GE facility outside Greenville, or transporting forest products and farming equipment downstate. The passenger station is long gone, and some of the spur lines are rusted out and covered with weeds. But in the sweltering summer of 1913, this was the spot where an angry mob hanged a man and left his body dangling from a rickety trestle over River Street.

Even before the assault on August 11, Richard Puckett— according to the papers, at least—was a Negro with a "bad reputation." As the story went, he was fresh off the county chain gang on the afternoon he leapt into the road and began dragging a white woman from her horse and buggy into the underbrush. The woman called out to her brothers, who were traveling along the same road in a separate carriage, and the "would-be rapist" lit off for the woods. Later that day, a search party apprehended Puckett and took him to the county jail.

As word of the attack spread from field hand to tenant

farmer, from domestic servant to drayman and finally to the businessmen in their downtown offices, a crowd began assembling on the square. By nightfall, more than one thousand people had crammed shoulder to shoulder in the narrow alleyways, kicking up clouds of dust, banging on the iron gates at North Caroline Street, hollering at the sheriff to bring the prisoner out. Shortly after ten o'clock, they stormed the jail. Armed with crowbars and sledgehammers, they clambered up a flight of stairs and broke down two steel doors to get at Puckett in his cell. They dragged the accused man through the square and down to the trestle, lobbed a twelve-foot length of rope over one of the crossbeams, and hoisted his body into the night air. Then they shot him, firing hundreds of rounds into their victim, an act the *Laurens Advertiser* later described as "the climax of an exciting day."

Puckett's body was left dangling among the laurels, but the townspeople returned the next morning to admire what they'd done. For avenging the woman—the papers never did release her name, but she was said to be a wealthy widow from a neighboring town—the governor praised "the good white people of Laurens County," who, he told reporters, never failed "to defend the honor and virtue of the women of their county and state."

Eleven African Americans were lynched in Laurens County between 1877 and 1950, but the Puckett murder is the one folks still talk about. If contemporaneous reports are to be believed, nearly half the town showed up that night; farmers and mill workers from farther afield were still arriving to join the lynch mob in the wee hours of the morning, long after the man was already dead. And though Puckett's body was cut down in the forenoon of the following day, a piece of the lynching rope was left dangling from the bridge. Maybe by accident. Maybe on purpose. Whatever the intent, nobody ever bothered to take the rope down—not as the civil rights movement came and went, nor as the schools were finally integrated in the fall of 1970, nor as marsh ferns and honeysuckle vines spiraled their way up the trestle pier and kudzu crept along the banks of River Street. For more than seven decades, the rope hung there, twisting in the breeze, a stark reminder of the horrors of the Jim Crow era.

"We used to walk under that trestle," said Reverend David Kennedy, who passed by the rope nearly every day as a child, each time he walked from Jersey, the largest of the historically black neighborhoods in Laurens, to the center of town. "And we heard stories. Whoever took that rope down, the same thing that happened to Richard Puckett was gonna happen to them."

The trestle was finally removed in the mid-1980s as part of a traffic flow project. But by then, the story of Richard Puckett's death was as much a part of the landscape as the smokestacks and water towers, the abandoned Laurens Glass factory where workers once fired thousands of bottles for the Coca-Cola company, or the grand homes presiding over West Main.

UNTIL THE AFTERNOON of March 1, 1996, not many people beyond the Upstate had heard of Laurens. Certainly the residents could not have anticipated the sudden influx of national attention. About the only sign of anything unusual at all had been the banging of hammers and the cutting of plywood, sounds of construction ringing out from the old Echo theater. But when the block letters were finally slid into the marquee, announcing the name of a new business, the Redneck Shop and "World's Only" KKK Museum; when the theater turned out to be owned by two proud Klansmen; when reporters started to descend on Laurens from New York and Washington and Los Angeles, then from as far away as Australia and Japan; when the courthouse square became the site of violent protests and general unrest, just about everyone in town claimed to have been blindsided.

"That's in the past," a woman from nearby Gray Court explained to the *Greenville News*. "If I thought about it much, it would bother me, but I try to keep my mind on the Bible."

Perhaps the only person who wasn't surprised by the sudden arrival of the Redneck Shop was Reverend David Kennedy. The Klan had been active in and around Laurens more or less since the days of Reconstruction—that was no secret—and every now and again, news of a cross left burning in someone's yard still made the local papers. Just three months earlier, a little church up the road, Jesus Christ Holy Gospel, had burned down under suspicious circumstances. But for Kennedy, that length of rotted rope had been the surest sign of trouble. Though nearly a century had passed since the lynching, hardly anyone in town had learned the truth of what happened that night: that Puckett was framed and murdered, his death hailed as a victory for the white race.

One by one, Kennedy would lead reporters away from the square, across the tracks, and on into Jersey, to the place where River Street descends into a swampy marsh. "America would love to put all the blame on the Ku Klux Klan," he'd tell them, cutting a path through the saplings. "But what creates this atmosphere that allows the Klan to become *bold?*" He would then point to a spot in the middle distance, the place where his great-great-uncle died for a crime he didn't commit, and explain that the rope had always been a warning.

Racism, he often told his parishioners, is a strange organism. A living thing. You can trim the branch, you can try to cut it out by the root, you can bury it deep in the ground and deprive it of light. But when the conditions are right, it blooms.

one

THE MASK THAT GRINS
AND LIES

FEBRUARY 1996

Reverend David Kennedy stood in his shirtsleeves at the edge of
the pasture, studying the police officer loping toward him across
the grass. The man was tall and lanky, hair close-cropped and
side-parted, and he had a kind of hangdog manner about him—
the way he rolled his shoulders forward and tucked his chin to
his chest, as if trying to render himself invisible. The cop flicked
away the butt of his cigarette, and Kennedy watched the glowing ember streak across the dark. A wind kicked up, bowing the
trees. Kennedy crossed his arms against his chest and shivered.

"They see me talkin to you, Rev, and they gon terminate
me," the cop said, extending his hand. "But I got to share this
with you."

Kennedy had recognized the officer's voice when he called
earlier that afternoon—the reedy quality, the cowboy cadence.
Calls like these weren't altogether unusual; cops and reverends
tend to weave in and out of each other's lives in small towns,
brushing past one another in the city jail or milling around together in the marble halls of the county courthouse. Kennedy

knew just about everybody in the Laurens City Police and the
Laurens County Sheriff's Office. Quite a few state troopers, too.
What made this call unusual had been the officer's request to
speak with the reverend alone, someplace private. "Safe," actually, was the word he had used, and this was the spot Kennedy
had chosen, a plot of brown pasture beneath a towering oak tree
adjacent to the Beasley Mortuary, a black-owned funeral parlor
in the southernmost reaches of Jersey. About the safest spot in
town for a white cop who didn't want to be seen.

"You can share it with me," Kennedy said. "It won't go nowhere." The reverend was a garrulous man by nature, but he
spoke now in the practiced, almost detached manner of a priest
taking confession. Not too eager, never excited. Almost aloof.

"You can't tell no one," the officer said.

"I won't."

"I know I can trust you. That's why I called you."

Kennedy gave an almost imperceptible nod and waited.

"I saw some stuff," the cop said finally, shaking his head.
He glanced over his shoulder, lowered his voice, and shoved his
hands into the pockets of his windbreaker. "I found out what
they're doin at the old Echo theater."

Exactly what had been going on at the Echo was a question folks in Laurens had been putting to themselves for several
months. It was under new ownership, that much seemed certain, and some kind of renovation or refurbishment was under
way. But whatever was going on, it was being kept a total mys-
tery, a closely guarded secret. There had been no signage on the
doors, no "Grand Opening" announcements in the local papers.
The windows were dark and papered over.

Kennedy hadn't so much as stepped foot inside the Echo in
nearly three decades, which was about how long the theater
had been closed. As a boy, he'd preferred the Harlem theater,

the movie house for black patrons over on Back Street, a small African American business district just east of the square. At the Harlem, he could watch the westerns he loved, *Shane* or the Billy the Kid flicks, without the indignity of having to enter through a side door and trudge upstairs to the colored balcony, without being hollered at for talking too much or having the audacity to laugh "too loudly."

One day when he was ten or eleven, however, Kennedy convinced his mother to let him go to the movies all by himself, for the very first time. An Elvis picture was showing at the Capitol—the Echo's sister theater, on the south side of the square. David bought his ticket and purchased a soda and found a seat in the balcony. Halfway through the film, around the time Elvis finished crooning "Puppet on a String," David shimmied out of his row, approached the white man who'd sold him his ticket, and asked for directions to the men's room.

"He wouldn't tell me," Kennedy remembered, years later. "I said, 'There's nowhere we could use the restroom?' He said no."

If Kennedy was angry or confused, those feelings quickly gave way to a more pressing emotion: panic. He had to relieve himself. *Now.* But finding a secluded spot somewhere outside, mere steps from the courthouse and City Hall and the police station, was out of the question. He thought fleetingly of making a run for the Back Street, but he knew he'd never make it in time. So instead, with a kind of sickening realization of the inevitable, he tiptoed back to the balcony, sat as far away from everyone else as he could manage, and tied a sweater around his waist to cover the growing wet spot on his trousers. The minute the house lights went up, he bolted.

"I hit that door real fast, and ran home. *That's* how I remember the Capitol theater."

For a black child growing up in the Jim Crow South, the

Echo and the Capitol were one and the same—both located on the courthouse square, both operated by the same proprietor, and both seemingly designed to humiliate you in your otherness. They were shuttered around the same time, too, in the mid-1960s, amid growing competition from drive-in theaters and the rising popularity of television, though Kennedy had not been particularly sad to see either of them go. Over the coming decades, retail businesses would sometimes take up residence in the former lobby of the Capitol, but for some reason the Echo was never included in the city's revitalization plans, never benefited from the public-private funds raised back in the 1980s to improve the historic district. The building and all of its contents—projector, screen, concessions equipment—were sold at auction in 1989, but still the theater sat empty, slipping further and further into a state of disrepair. Until the construction started, it seemed as though the Echo might be vacant forever.

"What'd you see?" Kennedy asked the officer. "What's the problem?"

The cop shifted his weight from foot to foot. From beyond the tree line came the whining blast of a CSX freight engine. "At first I thought it was just 'sposed to be a southern pride thing. Confederate-flag T-shirts and license plates and all that. But then I started lookin around."

Kennedy listened with growing interest, and then something closer to disgust, as the officer described the merchandise displayed inside the theater's lobby: Maltese and Celtic cross patches lined up in rotating display racks, just like postcards; vintage WHITES ONLY placards and segregation-era signs; T-shirts and bumper stickers emblazoned with all manner of racist invective. The walls were lined with photos of cross burnings and Klan rallies. In the center of the room was a slender mannequin, the kind you might find in a ladies' dress shop, outfitted in a Klansman's hood and robe.

"I reckon they'll open for business any day." The cop shook his head again, in sadness or in resignation. "I don't know what's going on in Laurens."

It was obvious now why the officer had called him: Reverend Kennedy's reputation as a local civil rights leader. He'd built his congregation, New Beginning Missionary Baptist, from the ground up, and he'd founded the Laurens County Soup Kitchen, through which members of his congregation served an average of 1,500 meals each week. He knew, had heard of, or was related to just about everybody in Laurens. A simple crosstown errand could stretch to the better part of three hours, since he felt compelled to stop and chat with almost everyone he happened to pass on the way. He was quick with a hug and known for delivering one of his trademark phrases: "hallelujah up there" if the word was good, or a reminder to "pump it up for Jesus!" for someone down on his luck. He was used to taking calls at all hours of the day and night, to receiving visitors unannounced at the church and at his home, and to providing assistance to people seeking all manner of favors.

Granted, the wisdom he dispensed these days tended to have less of a spiritual nature and be more concerned with matters of practical guidance. Help for a parishioner facing the threat of eviction. The name of a sympathetic lawyer or bail bondsman. Lately he'd been called more and more to help with the most basic of needs, especially food. David Kennedy kept stockpiles of food so that he'd always have something to offer—collards, okra, loaves of white bread, canned fruit, all of it donated from area businesses or members of his congregation and then tucked into the closet in his office or the trunk of his car. Every day he struggled to live his faith: *blessed are the poor and the hungry, blessed are they who are persecuted.* He served as coordinator of the local minority rights group, Project Awakening, and as a staff member at the Carolina Alliance for Fair Employment. Over the last ten years, he'd organized protests and marched alongside local and state-level politicians, never failing to speak out against prejudice and hate. But as he watched the cop climb back into his car and head off down Harper Street, an uneasy feeling came over him.

"That cop was nervous," he said later. "I can see him now, just shaking."

Reverend Kennedy was born in his grandparents' house, in the Brown Franklin Court Negro housing project, in the summer of 1953. Of course, he wasn't a reverend then—it would be eighteen years before he received his call to ministry. In those days, he was just David, the first child born to John Henry and Mary Frances "Frankie" Kennedy, but already part of a large, boisterous, close-knit family that had lived in Laurens and the surrounding rural area for generations.

Back then, the "projects" were still new, constructed after the Housing Act of 1949 initiated a sweeping expansion of the federal government's role in public housing. David, along with his parents and grandparents and a revolving cast of aunts, uncles, and cousins, lived at C-51 Spring Street—"C" for "colored," though the label was hardly necessary, as the projects were rigorously segregated. Low-income white families lived on the west side of the complex in what were called the Henry Laurens Homes, in honor of the town's namesake. (Born in 1724, Henry

Laurens had been president of the Second Continental Congress and a partner in Austin and Laurens, the largest slave trading house in North America.) Black residents, meanwhile, were situated exclusively to the east, at the bottom of a low hill. Aside from the crude alphanumeric distinction, the housing tracts were alike in virtually every way—row upon row of single-story redbrick homes, with backyards that butted up against each other to form long, grassy alleyways—split into perfect halves by Spring Street. For black residents, Spring Street was the proverbial line in the sand, the line you did not cross. And in that way, the projects served as a kind of microcosm of the larger community.

In the late 1800s, after Reconstruction gave way to Jim Crow, after they were stripped of political power and basic civil rights, African Americans in Laurens began to carve out their own unique spaces: On the north side of town, just beyond the courthouse square, the neighborhoods of Sunset Park, Rich Hill, and Stumptown sprang up around the town's first two black churches, St. Paul First Baptist and Bethel AME. By the early 1900s, a thriving business district—the Back Street—developed just east of downtown, filled with groceries, restaurants, barbershops, fish and meat markets, and pool halls that catered almost exclusively to black residents. The rest of town, however, remained lily-white. And with the color lines thus drawn, the white residents in Laurens went about their daily lives, heeding a social order both cruel and duplicitous.

In the Wattsville section of town, white patrons kept Bell's Café packed from sunup to sundown, even though everyone knew that the food—cornbread, collards, black-eyed peas, potato salad, fried chicken—was prepared exclusively by black women. (Black patrons could purchase food, too, provided they entered and exited through the back door and ate their meals standing up in the parking lot.) David's grandfather often came home from work talking about a white man, Clyde Francis, who at lunchtime didn't much mind eating in the company of his black coworkers so long as he had a physical object—a brick, usually—to set down in the dirt, a crude way of delineating the color line himself. And while it would have been unthinkable to eat in the same restaurant or drink from the same water fountain, white families regularly brought black women into the intimate functions of their homes: hiring them to cook their meals, launder their clothes, and care for their babies. Even some of the poorest whites in Laurens could still afford black domestic labor.

"Oh, God, it was cheap," said Samuel Shipman, whose own home didn't have indoor plumbing until he reached the age of nine or ten. "My neighbor was a half textile worker, half farmer. He had some property and he had a family of three living on his property. They didn't earn any money, just sharecropping food. They'd call him 'Massa Craig' and they took his last name."

Perhaps what's most jarring about Shipman's recollection is that he wasn't talking about race relations at the turn of the century. He was describing Laurens in the 1950s.

Even in the Kennedy home, there were lines you did not cross. Because David's parents worked most days, including the weekends, he was often cared for by members of his extended family. The patriarch, however, the undisputed head of the household, was David's grandfather. "He was a powerhouse," Kennedy says. "Not a mean man, but a serious guy. Everybody respected him." At dinnertime, the notion of even *looking* at a fork before his grandfather had blessed the meal was as unthinkable as the prospect of loitering around the homes on West Main.

But no matter how steadfastly black residents adhered to the racial etiquette of the day, the color line was readily—and frequently—crossed by white residents.

"Now, I'm going to speak the language of the time," Shipman recalled, with some measure of regret. "We'd go 'nigger-knocking.' You know, get in the back of a pickup truck with a broom, go down to the black section of town, and ride around, just swatting them with a broom. And go down by the railroad tracks and pick up stones and throw at them. It was a game."

For whites who lived in the Henry Laurens Homes, playing that game was as easy as crossing over Spring Street. On one such afternoon, when David was perhaps six or seven years old, a group of white teenagers crested the hill, each with a hand tucked in the fly of his trousers.

"They were coming down the road with their penises out," he said. "Just laughing, telling us, 'Come and get it. I got this for ya.' So of course the black kids were all upset. And I said, 'I'm going to tell my grandfather!' My powerful grandfather."

Back at the house, he waited patiently as his grandfather pulled on his overalls, shuffled out onto the front porch, and leveled an icy stare in the boys' direction. David, however, had been expecting a little more fire and brimstone. After a few moments of steely silence, he tugged on the leg of his grandfather's pants. "Pop? What ya gonna do?"

The answer, of course, was nothing. David was too young to understand that if you were black, challenging the color line was mortally dangerous. Only a year or two earlier, in the summer of 1957, a Laurens County sharecropper had been shot to death by his landlord for refusing to work on the afternoon of the Fourth of July. (The landlord, despite admitting to the murder, was promptly acquitted.) So David was left with a profound sense of disappointment. And at the dinner table that night, while everyone else bowed their heads in prayer, he came to a crushing realization: his grandfather was just a man—a *black* man, at that—and not nearly as powerful as he'd imagined.

By THE EARLY 1960s, David's family had moved out of the projects and into a modest home in Jersey, a little house they heated with wood and coal in the wintertime, with a yard full of peach and pear trees—a step-up attributable to the hours his parents spent performing backbreaking labor. Frankie bounced from one factory job to the next, while David's father, John, worked the third shift at Laurens Glass (midnight to 8:00 a.m.) before heading out to various construction sites to lay brick for another eight hours. Amid their busy work schedules, they found time to have three more children: two girls, Belinda and Pamela, and a boy, Ralph (which in the Kennedy drawl sounds more like "Rav"), named for a prominent local businessman with an office over on the Back Street.

David had always been a serious, independent child. Ralph, on the other hand, was rambunctious and silly and effusive with his affection. According to family lore, he once reached out and plucked a bird from the air in midflight, a feat the Kennedys considered practically biblical. Elders in the community, evidently charmed by his gentle nature, routinely gifted Ralph with jam and biscuits and cookies, often enough that David sometimes wondered, *Why for him and not for me?* The year the boys were given matching suits—church clothes—Ralph modeled his to great fanfare; all the aunts and uncles went crazy talking about how sharp he looked, making such a fuss that David eventually turned to his mother and quietly asked, "Don't we have the same kinda suit?"

Despite Ralph's special place within the family, there was no rivalry between the boys. David was extremely protective of his brother and sisters, which may just have been *his* nature, perhaps bolstered by his religious upbringing. David's grandfather was a deacon, his grandmother taught Sunday school, and though his parents often worked on Sundays, David attended services at Springfield Baptist each and every week, without exception. "I *wanted* to go," he said later. "I was raised in the church. And I loved hearing the Bible stories. I can still remember my grandmother teachin 'bout Moses. I loved hearing about the little baby in the basket."

The story had particular resonance for David. Moses's people, the Israelites, were enslaved and oppressed by the ruler of Egypt. Concerned that his subjects might one day rise up against him—"Behold, the people of the children of Israel are more and mightier than we . . . let us deal with them, lest they multiply" (Exodus 1:9–10)—Pharaoh commanded that all male Hebrew children be killed at birth. But Moses's mother could not bear the death of her infant son, so she placed him in a basket and concealed him in the bushes along the banks of the Nile.

"I was just fascinated by that," Kennedy said. "I think it bothered me that a baby was in trouble, that someone wanted to kill an innocent baby. Of all the stories and all the Sunday school lessons, that's the one I remember most vividly. And when I think about it now, most of my fights have been for people who been in trouble."

The move to Jersey may have offered David a bit of a reprieve from the prowling teens in the Henry Laurens Homes, but in the early 1960s there was no escaping his otherness. David was reminded of it constantly: when he whistled at a pretty young white girl and his mother slapped him so hard that he can still recall the sting of her hand on his thigh. It was there every time he was made to use a side door or a back entrance, every time someone shouted at him or called him a "nigger." He took refuge in the love of his family. The church, meanwhile, provided a sense of order, not to mention something of a safe haven. But in the spring of 1963, everything changed.

David was in the fourth grade, walking across the campus of his elementary school, when a friend rushed to his side. "Dave! Your brother—he got hit by a car. He's dead."

David was so profoundly disoriented by the news that his natural response was to attack. He dropped his books and took off in a full sprint, rearing back his right arm to deliver a mighty punch. "I really got delirious in the head. I was running at him to fight him, for telling me that. For talking about my brother like that. And he kept trying to calm me down, saying, 'Don't fight me, Dave.'"

It wasn't until hours later, after being reunited with his family, that David began to piece together the details of his brother's death. That morning, Ralph and his mother had taken a cab uptown to visit with the boys' uncle, and Ralph had been so characteristically excited and exuberant that as soon as the taxi pulled to the curb, he leapt out the back door and dashed around the rear of the vehicle, into the street. Seconds later, while Frankie was busy paying the fare, Ralph was struck broadside by a 1956 Pontiac. He died three hours later at Laurens District Hospital.

He had been six years old. David was nine.

Frankie was so overcome with grief she had to be hospitalized. The day of the funeral, David's grandmother and grandfather and aunts huddled around her bed, trying to calm her down enough so that she might attend her son's burial. She was inconsolable, however, and at some point she cried out, "Lord, have mercy on me."

David, crouched at his mother's bedside, reached for her hand. "He will, Mama, if you let him."

"I shall never forget that," Frankie said later. "I shall *never* forget him telling me that."

MAYBE IT WAS losing his brother so young, maybe it was what happened with his grandfather that day in the projects, maybe it was just the way David Kennedy was wired, but as he grew into adolescence, he became incapable of standing idly by in the face of injustice. When confronted with unfair treatment or immoral behavior, David simply refused to keep his mouth shut.

By high school he had earned the nickname "Vamp"—as in vampire, a cruel reference to the oddity of his smile. (Rather than treat an abscess, David's dentist had opted to pull several of the boy's front teeth instead.) Before long, however, that nickname evolved to "Revolutionary Vamp." It was by then the late 1960s, the height of the black power movement; James Brown's "Say It Loud (I'm Black and I'm Proud)" had just rocketed to the top of the charts, and for perhaps the first time, David and his friends were starting to feel a real sense of pride in their heritage. "You just an invisible guy around here, Dave," one of his friends once told him. "But when a problem comes up, you come full glory."

Indeed, David had plenty of opportunities to shine, because in Laurens there was no shortage of things to protest. Though *Brown v. Board of Education* had outlawed "separate but equal" education back in 1954, the high court failed to provide specific instructions or guidelines, mandating only that school districts around the country begin the process of desegregating with "all deliberate speed." The ambiguity of that language left the door wide open for misapplication. Fifteen years later, most schools across the South were still practicing de facto segregation. In Laurens, a handful of black students had matriculated at the otherwise all-white high school, but the majority of African Americans attended Sanders High, which, like most Negro schools, was chronically underfunded. David and his friends studied using hand-me-down books, outdated editions cast off by the white schools. The Sanders marching band performed in hand-me-down uniforms. The football team played in hand-me-down gear, which was so woefully inadequate that the boys resorted to shoving socks under their shoulder pads and wrapping dishrags around their knees.

"We were tired of hand-me-downs," David says. "We wanted something new."

To make up for the lack of official funding, soon-to-be graduates raised money for a senior class gift, leaving behind the means to buy a scoreboard for the basketball gym, new football jerseys, or whatever else might be in high demand. And that worked fine for a while, until some ambiguity sprang up about where, exactly, the bulk of the money was going. Because right around the same time each and every year, the principal at Sanders would suddenly be driving a brand-new car. "We knew what was going on," Kennedy said. "But no one would say anything. No one would challenge him."

No one, that is, except David. Sometime during his junior year, he walked right up to the principal during a break between classes and very calmly expressed his concerns straight to the man's face: "I think we have a right to know what you do with the money we raise."

"And *that* was the beginning of my end," he said later.

David had always been too slight and too small for athletics, but his position as head trainer of the football program earned him a leadership role and a sense of camaraderie, not to mention a ticket to get out of town every other week. At practice on the afternoon after he confronted the principal, however, one of the coaches pulled him aside. David had been fired. "It shattered my whole world," he said. "I was very depressed."

His depression was short-lived, thankfully. At the insistence of another coach—a white coach—David was soon reinstated. But the run-in with the principal had two lasting effects: it bolstered his willingness to speak out, and it earned him one heck of a reputation among his peers. Everyone at Sanders came to understand that "Revolutionary Vamp" was feisty and fearless, a person you could rely on in times of trouble.

David was no less outspoken in the fall of 1971, the start of his senior year, when it was announced that the Laurens County School District would finally undergo mandatory integration. Instead of graduating from Sanders, a more-than-fifty-year-old pillar of the black community, he would be forced to matriculate at Laurens High. And though integration in Laurens proved less violent than in other areas of the state—a hundred miles to the east, for example, rioters in Lamar pelted three school buses carrying black students with rocks and bricks, shattered the windows with ax handles, and overturned two buses before succumbing to teargas—for David and his classmates, losing the school they had called their own still proved traumatic. "We lost our mascot," Kennedy said. "We lost our colors. We lost our alma mater. Black teachers lost their jobs. Black administrators were demoted or fired. They tried to take the Sanders name from us, too." (Indeed, the county's original plan was to transform Sanders High, named after the first black principal of the town's first Negro school, into Laurens Middle. The plan was abandoned only after loud and sustained protests by the black community.)

All that year, David and his friends endured everything from minor slights in the classroom—David *hated* that one of his new teachers insisted on referring to her black students, pejoratively, as "y'all"—to more consequential forms of discrimination. And in response, David continued to earn his nickname: organizing walkouts, storming the principal's office every few weeks with some new list of complaints. "It was not popular here, for anybody in Laurens—a town that's named after an eighteenth-century slave trader—to speak out. But I didn't understand the fear. I became angry at the fear. I always thought the white guys should be challenged. If people don't talk, this kinda thing will keep going on and on."

By the time he graduated, David had made quite a name for himself. Yet he had no intention of furthering his education or his activism. Instead, his father got him a job at Laurens Glass, and he supplemented his meager income by raking leaves or painting houses or hopping cars at the Carolina drive-in. And he likely would've continued on like that, working as a low-wage laborer for decades, had he not attended a meeting with the formidable new president of Benedict College, in the fall of 1971, that changed his life.

Benjamin Payton had grown up in Orangeburg, South Carolina, one of nine children born to an impoverished rural minister and farmer, before embarking on an improbably illustrious career. In 1955, he earned a bachelor's degree in sociology from South Carolina State University, and then took a veritable tour of the Ivy League, earning a second bachelor's (in divinity) from Harvard, a master's in philosophy from Columbia, and a doctorate in ethics from Yale. He later became a major figure in the civil rights movement, helping to organize the 1963 March on Washington and the 1965 march in Selma. Then, at the ripe old age of thirty-three, he became president of Benedict, a his-

torically black, Baptist-affiliated liberal arts college in Columbia. Payton was a tireless advocate for African Americans and a
gifted public speaker, so when he showed up in Laurens—to address a public meeting of the local NAACP at New Grove Baptist Church—he arrived to a packed house. And young David,
perhaps recognizing something of himself in Payton, was elec-
trified. "He spellbound me," Kennedy said. "He spellbound my
best friend. You see somebody with courage, who tells it like it
is? I said, 'Man! I am going to Benedict!'"

Which is exactly what he did. Though he hadn't told many
people, by then Kennedy had had a religious experience—a calling to ministry. After receiving his family's blessing, he enrolled
at Benedict in the fall of 1972 to study religion and philosophy.

David thrived at Benedict. In fact, in some ways it was as
if the school had been founded with exactly him in mind: its
original mission, before expanding into a four-year college
with a variety of degree programs, was to train African American "teachers and preachers" and to prepare young men and
women to become "forces for good" in society. By the time he
graduated—magna cum laude—David had served as a member
of the school's Judiciary Board and Religious Planning Committee, president of the Pre-Theological Society, and treasurer
of the Alpha Kappa Mu Honor Society. He'd also managed to
meet a pretty young schoolteacher from Laurens, Janice Press-
ley, and before heading off to pursue a graduate degree from the
Divinity School at Vanderbilt University, David married her at
Springfield Baptist, surrounded in love by an enormous wedding party: fifteen bridesmaids and fifteen groomsmen.

Two months later, David and his new wife arrived in Nashville to find a campus shaped, scalded, and in many ways made
wiser by the civil rights movement. Back in 1960, an African

American divinity student, James Lawson, had been expelled for organizing local lunch counter sit-ins and teaching forms of nonviolent resistance to segregation; most of the Divinity School faculty resigned in protest, and the "Lawson Affair" quickly mushroomed into a PR disaster, spawning nationwide demonstrations, tarnishing the school's reputation, and jeopardizing the university's funding. "It was a defining event, and still is," Eugene TeSelle, a retired Divinity School professor, explained to *Vanderbilt Magazine* in 2002. "In a sense, Vanderbilt was lucky to have had this crisis at this period in history—the University learned how to deal with conflict—and it was lucky to have weathered it."

By the time David arrived in the fall of 1976, the Divinity School had adopted a decidedly liberal tone, attracted new high-profile professors, and published a series of commitments to racial equality and social justice in the annual catalog—all direct results of the Lawson Affair. In class and around campus, David was very much in his element, studying and debating and preaching about the intersection of race, religion, and faith. Jan, meanwhile, bore the first of the couple's three children while pursuing a master's from Georgia Peabody College for Teachers. The couple gave their daughter—and later their sons—African names: 'Lola, meaning "wealth and abundance"; Adedeji, "our joy has doubled"; and Akil Andwele, "God has brought me." In his spare time, David worked as a youth coordinator at Edgehill United Methodist Church, a progressive mixed-race congregation led by pastor Bill Barnes, an affordable-housing advocate. He carved out a place for himself within a vibrant spiritual community.

But then Jan's grandparents, who had raised her from infancy, fell ill.

"I didn't want to come back home," Kennedy said. "I told Jan, 'If I go back, I won't have peace.'"

And yet he realized just how much being away from Laurens had taken a toll on his wife. Jan desperately missed her family, her aunts and uncles and cousins. Her grandparents were dying. And so the Kennedys returned to South Carolina. "It's one of the regrets of my life," he said.

SEVEN YEARS LATER, in October 1986, Rev. Kennedy was in the middle of his Wednesday-night Bible study when he noticed something strange. Midweek meetings were usually small gatherings, and with the Laurens County Fair in town that week he hadn't expected a particularly large turnout. Midway through his study, however—a discussion of slavery as metaphor in the book of Galatians—he looked up and realized he was suddenly preaching to a heck of a lot of people. "I thought, 'Wow! Look at all these people coming in to Bible study. That's really great.'" Feeling pleased with himself, he continued on with the lesson, but when dozens more people continued to stream in the door, nodding to one another and quietly finding seats near the back of the room, he knew something was definitely up. None of the church's events had ever approached anything close to standing room only.

"You know," he said to the crowd, cracking a smile, "I'm beginning to think you're not all here just for Bible study. What can I do for you?"

After a bit of prodding, one of the newcomers stepped forward. "We got some drug problems here, Rev, and we're worried about our community." The man went on to describe the proliferation of crack houses and front businesses in town, interrupted every so often by murmurs and shouts of "Amen" and "That's right!"

David knew the man was right. The Laurens he and his wife had come home to was not in great shape. As far back as the early 1970s, rural towns across South Carolina had reported sharp upticks in crime, much of it drug-related. By the mid-1980s, things had gone from bad to worse. In the neighboring town of Abbeville, cops had just completed their first-ever large-scale drug bust, serving forty-seven warrants for possession and distribution of marijuana and cocaine. About thirty miles to the west, rumors were flying that the Anderson County sheriff himself had been arrested on trafficking charges (a claim the sheriff vehemently denied, going so far as to offer a $1,000 reward for information regarding the source of the rumors). And in Laurens thirteen months prior, cops had made one of the biggest busts in the history of the state: twelve thousand pounds of marijuana, with a value estimated at $5 million, had been raided from a rural farm just fifteen miles south of the square. By September 1985, the State Law Enforcement Division's narcotics units had seized more than twice as many marijuana plants (forty-four thousand) as the previous year's total.

After returning to South Carolina in the late 1970s, Kennedy had bounced from rural church to rural church, each one seemingly poorer than the next. (A small congregation in Abbeville, he was dismayed to discover, had paid its previous pastor little more than $100 a week.) In the fall of 1984, he founded his own church, New Beginning Missionary Baptist, but to support his family he took whatever paying job he could find: working at Walmart for a while, then at various check-cashing companies. More recently, he'd become a corrections officer at Dutchman Correctional Institution, a brand-new 528-bed minimum-security facility in nearby Cross Anchor. The prison

population in the state—and across the country—was explod-
ing; President Reagan had just signed the Anti–Drug Abuse
Act, establishing lengthy mandatory minimums for drug-
related offenses. But the longer Rev. Kennedy worked in the
jails, the more convinced he became that cops were too focused
on small-time dealers and that many of the arrests were racially
motivated.

It wasn't a secret why so many folks from the community
had shown up at his doorstep. Despite his time away at college and the three years spent in Nashville, everyone still knew
Kennedy as a rabble-rouser, the kid who'd challenged his principal and organized walkouts during the days of integration. So
rather than fight against his reputation, Kennedy decided to put
it to work. At Sunday services, in City Council meetings—any
place he could be assured an audience—he started speaking out
about rising crime and local drug use, while insisting that black
men were disproportionately targeted and arrested. As he had
anticipated, this generated immediate pushback. Local reporters pointed out that of the forty-four drug-related arrests in
Laurens in 1985, twenty-three of those arrested were white and
twenty-one were black, and the mayor of Laurens, Bob Dominick, personally attended a meeting at New Beginning in order
to refute the claim. But Kennedy had a point. In addition to
draconian mandatory minimums, Reagan's Anti-Drug Act had
introduced the 100:1 crack-to-powder disparity. (Under new
laws, possession of five grams of crack cocaine, a cheaper vari-
ant favored by impoverished African Americans, would carry
the same sentence as five hundred grams of powder cocaine.)
It would take decades for policy experts to acknowledge how
crippling such laws were to the black community, and for lawmakers to reduce the disparity by passing the 2010 Fair Sentencing Act.

In November, less than a month after the impromptu meeting at his church, Kennedy decided to ramp up the pressure. At a community meeting, he stood up and publicly accused law enforcement officers of taking payoffs—another allegation he'd caught wind of—though he refused to name any names. (Sheriff Billy Robertson was reportedly so incensed that he almost stormed out of the meeting.) Then, in December, he started drumming up publicity for a newer, bigger event: a protest march, which would convene at the courthouse steps and snake right through the center of town.

Rev. Kennedy proved adept at courting the press. No fewer than three newspapers covered his plans, and though January 17 dawned dreary and bitter cold, he was ultimately pleased by the turnout: nearly a hundred people had gathered for the two-mile walk along West Main to the junior high school, including state senator Theo Mitchell and the Eighth Circuit Court solicitor Townes Jones. Even the mayor showed up. (The sheriff, not surprisingly, was a no-show.) At the rally afterward, Kennedy couldn't help but feel pleased: this was the kind of street-level ministry he'd once dreamed about, walking among his parishioners rather than hiding behind the pulpit. "I think people felt more secure just by meeting," he told reporters. "The people in the black community are filled with stories that you wouldn't believe. They just don't have the courage to come forth."

By the fall of 1988, Kennedy's focus had shifted from drug abuse awareness to exposing the practices of local law enforcement, in particular after the arrest of a well-known African American radio announcer. William Robertson—his on-air name was Kevin St. John—had been taken into custody after officers mistook him for a suspect in a knifing incident. When rumors began swirling that Robertson had been cuffed, threatened, and perhaps even physically assaulted, Rev. Kennedy promptly organized a series of protests. He also intensified his rhetoric, pledging to "turn the city upside down" and calling for a boycott of downtown businesses.

Over the coming months, each of Kennedy's marches and protests focused on broader and broader themes: police brutality, unfair policing of the black community, unfair hiring practices. And yet racial tensions in Laurens seemingly got worse—which is to say more visible. The local NAACP filed a lawsuit against the Laurens Commission of Public Works, seeking equal representation on its all-white board. A Laurens County parent, meanwhile, sued the school board for $10 million in punitive damages, alleging racial harassment and discrimination. "The catalyst for the entire situation was a day during Black History Month when [my son] asked to hear about things black people had done to make America great," she explained to the *Greenville News*. "His teacher told him they were already talking about it—slavery."

That merited a news conference from the courthouse steps. "We want to see justice done!" Kennedy thundered. "If we have to, we will encourage our children to boycott classes."

The ferocity of his message drew the ire of everyone from law enforcement officers to school officials, many of whom wondered if the outspoken reverend had finally gone too far. But then came the hanging.

In the wee hours of the morning on April 1, 1990, Edward James Cook—"Bobo" to his friends and family—was pulled over and arrested on a drunk driving charge. He was taken to the city jail and served breakfast in his cell at 6:45 a.m. Less than an hour and a half later, at 8:10, a prison guard found Cook with one end of a shirt wrapped around his neck, the other tied to an upper bunk. The coroner ruled Cook's death a suicide, and tensions in Laurens exploded.

One week after Cook's death, five hundred people crowded into the courthouse square, demanding answers. It was an enormous turnout for such a tiny town. The boy's own father made it clear to reporters that he didn't believe his son had killed himself. For more than an hour, Rev. Kennedy led protesters in songs and chants and cheers for equality. Despite the public outcry amid months of racial unrest, however, the Laurens City Police accepted no responsibility and offered no apology. After all, the autopsy had confirmed that Cook died by hanging, and the South Carolina State Law Enforcement Division (SLED) maintained that there was no evidence of foul play. So Rev. Kennedy did the only thing he could do: he protested again. Three times in less than three months. In response, the mayor complained to a local newspaper that Kennedy and his minority rights group—now going by the name Project Awakening— got "too upset about small issues."

"A black man died and this racist mayor calls it a small incident!" Kennedy shouted at his next demonstration.

It's hard to pinpoint exactly when Rev. Kennedy's relationship with the mayor went bad. Maybe it was when he'd called for a boycott of downtown businesses—Bob Dominick was himself a downtown business owner—or maybe the mayor's patience had just been tested one too many times. But when Dominick approached Kennedy's microphone and attempted to address the crowd, only to be drowned out by jeers and boos, something definitely changed. Now it was personal.

The protest had taken place on a Monday. The next day, Mayor Dominick stood before members of the City Council and prodded them to go on the record with their support for local law enforcement. "We've got some joker standing up on the courthouse steps making ugly remarks about us!" he said. "Sitting back making no comment is giving credit to what he is saying. We've got to stop putting our heads between our knees and acting like he isn't here." The approach, if melodramatic, appeared at least somewhat successful. Councilman Johnnie Bolt went so far as to say he was "completely impressed" with how things had been handled in the wake of Cook's death.

On Friday morning, however, Dominick decided that he'd like to have a word with the "joker" himself. Just before nine, he pulled into a strip mall parking lot north of the square—by then, Rev. Kennedy had resigned his position at Dutchman and was working at Quick Credit, a payday loan company—and confronted the reverend about a past-due community development loan. It was an odd piece of business for a town mayor, and particularly odd timing, since Kennedy had taken out the loan back in 1983. Kennedy immediately accused Dominick of racism, and the confrontation quickly turned violent. "He was right in my face—our noses were touching," Dominick later told reporters. According to witnesses, there was a fair amount of shoving and shouting and spitting on both sides. At some point, the mayor asked one of Kennedy's coworkers to call the police, but he left before the cops arrived. Rev. Kennedy, on the other hand, was taken into custody on charges of disorderly conduct and resisting arrest.

As the dispute played out in the press and public opinion started to turn against the mayor, officers of the municipal court decided the best course of action would be to drop all charges. "We knew there would be racial overtones the city could do without," city prosecutor Wyatt Saunders admitted to the *Greenville News*. Rev. Kennedy, however, was not about to sweep the incident under the rug. Instead, he opted for a jury trial.

"There was a black poet, Paul Lawrence Dunbar," he said, reflecting on the incident and his legacy in Laurens. "And he wrote: 'We wear the mask that grins and lies / It hides our cheeks and shades our eyes.' In other words, we have a face for white people and a face for black folk. But I refuse to wear a face. I'm just me all the time. And that disturbs a lot of people, especially black people. We were raised never to challenge anybody white. We were just supposed to pray and let God handle it. But I can't serve that kind of God."

two

A KERNEL OF TRUTH

A full ten years before Rev. Kennedy began questioning the suspicious circumstances of Bobo Cook's death, another South Carolina man was busy protesting a jail cell suicide. The cases themselves had striking similarities, but the men behind the protests had altogether different purposes. The year was 1980, and in the small town of Williamston, thirty-five miles northwest of Laurens, John Howard—an imperial officer of the Federated Knights of the Ku Klux Klan—was preparing to address a crowd of reporters outside the home of twenty-year-old Bobby Scroggs.

Like Cook, Scroggs had been arrested in early April on alcohol-related charges, in this case public intoxication and disorderly conduct. Like Cook, Scroggs had been found hanging by a shirt in his cell mere hours after he was taken into custody. And like Cook's death, the Scroggs suicide had triggered an immediate public outcry. But unlike the Cook case, there were no apparent racial implications—Scroggs was white, as were the arresting officer and the bulk of the local police force. Once the Klan got involved, however, tensions in Williamston rapidly escalated.

By Monday, April 7—two days after the boy's death—two large wooden crosses had been set ablaze on the outskirts of town. On Tuesday, a rowdy group of protesters gathered outside the Williamston Police Department, set fire to a pile of boxes and tires in the parking lot, and lobbed bottles and rocks at the firemen who arrived to put out the flames. The following Saturday, 150 people showed up at a Klan rally, where it was announced that a "Klan Bureau of Investigation," or KBI, would launch an official inquiry into the incident. Three more rallies took place over the next three weeks, leaving Williamston awash in racist propaganda and membership applications. Yet when it came time to reveal the findings of its "investigation," it appeared the KBI hadn't managed to uncover much of anything at all.

Dressed in a satin hood and robe, John Howard hemmed and hawed and evaded questions from the very reporters he'd asked to assemble on the boy's front lawn. He revealed no evidence, but hinted coyly that Scroggs might have been the victim of foul play, all before ending the press conference with a threat: if law enforcement failed to discover the "truth," he said, the Klan would return to reveal "all of the truth, all of the facts" gleaned during its probe.

Howard was a small man, no more than five foot six or five foot seven, with a round face and a flesh-colored mole on his forehead, right between his eyes. Friends and acolytes might describe him as calm, mild-mannered, even shy. But in front of a crowd, Howard came alive. Prone to long monologues about the origins of the Klan and the history of the South, he frequently—and effortlessly—whipped himself into a red-faced fervor. In a voice dripping with Carolina twang, he could talk a blue streak when his audience was receptive, thundering on about the dangers of "race mixing" and "mongrelization," but he was savvy enough to change tack if he sensed that a listener had his doubts.

Still, the Scroggs suicide was an odd cause célèbre for a white supremacist organization. In fact, most of the cops in Williamston viewed the Klan's sudden involvement as nothing more than an elaborate recruiting drive, a cheap play for money and publicity. And it wouldn't be the last time that Howard and his associates were accused of exploiting tragedy and ginning up intrigue for nothing more than their own personal gain.

JOHN HOWARD WAS born in Spartanburg in 1946 and raised in Laurens. He was the youngest of six children, just fifteen when his father, John Senior, died at the age of sixty-eight after a long illness. By eighteen he had married his first wife and fathered the first of three children. It should have been a happy time, but the young Howard was increasingly unsettled by the changes taking place in the world around him—by the sit-ins and bus boycotts, by the riots in Detroit and New York and Los Angeles, all of which played out nightly on his television. Years later, he would explain to the *Clinton Chronicle* that the civil unrest had "scared" him. But in interviews with journalist Patsy Sims, author of the 1978 book *The Klan*, he portrayed himself as having been a little more proactive: "I reached out and started searchin for an organization that could do somethin about the situation," he said.

The "situation" to which Howard referred was the sweeping social change at the heart of the civil rights movement. And the organization he found was the Ku Klux Klan. In the mid-1960s, the largest group operating in the South—boasting any-where from 25,000 to 35,000 members—was the United Klans of America, Knights of the Ku Klux Klan, Inc. (UKA), head-quartered in Tuscaloosa, Alabama, and led by a young salesman named Robert Shelton.

Shelton had joined a decade earlier, risen quickly through the ranks, and in just four short years as Imperial Wizard—or national leader—transformed the fledgling UKA into the larg-est white supremacist organization in the country, and also one of the deadliest. Between 1961 and 1965, members of the UKA and its affiliates were linked to, accused of, or indicted for a range of heinous crimes—assaulting Freedom Riders as they traveled through the segregated South, murdering a white civil rights worker during the Selma-to-Montgomery marches, bombing the Sixteenth Street Baptist Church (resulting in the deaths of four African American children).

It's unlikely that John Howard was a party to any such vi-olence. In its heyday, the UKA was most powerful in North Carolina, where Grand Dragon (or statewide leader) Bob Jones had amassed a veritable army—well over ten thousand Klans-men, by some estimates—divided into hundreds of individual chapters, called klaverns. South Carolina was a considerably smaller operation, and membership plummeted not long after John Howard took his oath. Beginning in the winter of 1965, a series of public hearings conducted by the House Un-American Activities Committee would reveal embarrassing evidence of fraud and mismanagement of Klan funds at the highest levels. Six of the most visible leaders were ultimately cited for con-tempt of Congress (for refusing to turn over membership rolls and financial documents). Shelton, Jones, and Robert Scoggin,

Grand Dragon of South Carolina, were each sentenced to a year in prison.

It was hardly the end of the United Klans, but the HUAC hearings took a massive toll on Shelton's hooded order. Hundreds of Klansmen were unmasked, the existence and locations of "secret" klaverns were revealed, and the months of unflattering front-page coverage sparked a fair bit of infighting. Shelton, who vowed to continue running the Klan from the confines of a federal jail cell, banished scores of members he deemed disruptive or viewed as competition (and a few who turned out to be longtime FBI informants). Thousands more resigned of their own accord.

One can only speculate why John Howard didn't hang up his robe, too. Perhaps the waning membership and sudden shortage of rallies left him restless. More likely is that belonging to the Klan gave him a sense of purpose. After traveling the country for three months, interviewing and interacting with hundreds of Klansmen for her book, Sims speculated that many had joined for reasons beyond racism: a need to belong, to feel important, to brighten drab lives, to be accepted.

In any case, after a brief tenure with the UKA, Howard readily switched allegiances to Robert Scoggin, who'd founded a group of his own after his release from prison in 1969. "United Klans wasn't doin anything," Howard explained to Sims. "They were interested in one thing—money. So I entered in with Mr. Scoggin."

FEW GROUPS OCCUPY such an outsized, almost mythical place in America's collective consciousness as the Ku Klux Klan. The eerie alliterative quality of the name, the conical white hat and

flowing robe, and the fiery cross have all become potent symbols of domestic terrorism and virulent hate. While many associate the KKK with pro-segregationist vigilantism in the rural
South, however, the Klan has actually had three distinct movements; its third and current iteration—which sprang up in the
1950s and '60s—is not a singular entity at all, but rather dozens
and dozens of splinter cells and rival factions operating under
endless variations on the name: the United Klans; the Invisible
Empire, Knights of the Ku Klux Klan; the White Knights of
the Ku Klux Klan; the Keystone Knights of the Ku Klux Klan;
et cetera. Each new fracture or faction adds yet another layer to
a long and complicated history, already rife with legend, myth,
and propaganda.

Talk to any Klansman today, and he'll likely tell you the
group was originally formed in order to protect defenseless
white southerners from marauding bands of "scalawags" and
"carpetbaggers" in the wake of the Civil War. In the twisted
version of history that John Howard preached to prospective
recruits, Confederate veterans had been so vilified and de-
based they "could not walk on the sidewalk . . . they walked in
the road, and they had to bow their heads in reverence to the
blacks," thousands of whom were "left in the South to rule and
dictate the southern white people." According to a report from
the Klanwatch Project of the Southern Poverty Law Center,
however, it was boredom—rather than any purported sense of
honor—that inspired six Confederate veterans to form a social
club in Pulaski, Tennessee, in the winter of 1865.* A *secret* club,

---

* That the original Klan was formed for purposes of entertainment, as a salve
for boredom, has long been historical consensus—but that doesn't mean the
birth of the Klan was entirely "innocent," or that its founders were without racial
prejudice. In her 2015 book *Ku-Klux: The Birth of the Klan During Reconstruction*, historian Elaine Frantz Parsons points out that race relations in Pulaski

to "heighten the amusement of the thing," with a range of titles and offices, from the Grand Wizard to the Grand Cyclops to the Grand Dragon, outrageous names chosen for a clear purpose: to be as "preposterous-sounding as possible." They called themselves the Ku Klux Klan, a play on the Greek word *kuklos*, meaning circle, and the Scottish *clan*, representing a kinship or brotherhood.

The robes—sheets and pillowcases at first, likely donned on impulse for a spur-of-the-moment ride through town—were likewise part of the silliness and "fun." But then the original six began to initiate new members, and what may well have started out as a postwar diversion morphed into something much more sinister.

The Klan was less than a year old, and Andrew Johnson barely a year into his presidency, when in 1866 the Radical Republicans won supermajorities in both houses of Congress. As a statesman, Johnson had proved a mass of contradictions. An avowed racist and slave-owner, he was nevertheless a rabid supporter of the Union—the only southern congressman, in fact, who remained loyal to the North even in the throes of war. Upon ascending to the presidency, however, Johnson seemingly reversed course, adopting a wildly lenient policy toward the southern states. He advocated zero protections for newly freed slaves and proposed virtually no repercussions for ex-Confederate rebels. Most provocative were the so-called black

---

were particularly fraught. Violent clashes between whites and freedpeople were common. Spontaneous rioting—and, later, organized violence—was already taking place across the South. It's certainly possible that some (or even all) of the founders committed acts of violence against freedpeople, too, but not as part of a secret, vigilante movement. From its founding through the spring of 1867, Parsons writes, "Ku-Klux members . . . did nothing to differentiate themselves from other white social and fraternal orders of the time."

codes, newly enacted state laws that severely restricted the rights of African Americans to own property, to vote, to carry weapons, to travel freely. For the slightest infraction—loitering, vagrancy, the "crime" of not having a job—blacks were arrested and forced into unpaid labor, work that largely resembled the "unpaid labor" they had performed before the war. With Johnson's tacit approval, the southern states were, in effect, reinstituting slavery.

That changed after the 1866 election. The Radicals, having amassed enough votes in Congress to override Johnson's vetoes, rammed through the Fourteenth and Fifteenth Amendments (granting citizenship and voting rights to former slaves), dismantled the newly formed southern state governments, and organized fair elections, which resulted in a number of black citizens assuming local and even national office. By 1868, Johnson would become the first-ever president to be impeached.

Meanwhile, many white southerners, perhaps most, abhorred the policies that came to be known as Radical Reconstruction. Duly elected black legislators were dismissed as illiterate, ignorant, venal. In South Carolina, conservatives lamented the "Africanization" of their state. And the Klan, which by then had attracted hundreds if not thousands of members, began its transition from social club to political terrorist group. In April or May 1867, representatives from the various chapters gathered in Nashville and reportedly elected the respected Confederate general Nathan Bedford Forrest to be their first Grand Wizard, or national leader.* It's widely believed that Forrest himself dis-

---

* That an organizational meeting of some kind took place in Nashville in the spring of 1867 and that this meeting was significant in terms of the Klan's transformation into a political entity remains the most commonly held view among historians. However, it is possible—even likely—that accounts of said meeting

banded the Klan just two years later, when the violence had so escalated that klaverns began to war with one another. It's *also* thought that Forrest may have only pretended to dissolve the order as a way of avoiding responsibility or personal retribution. Regardless, whatever commands Forrest may or may not have issued to his "troops" did nothing to quell the growing violence.

In towns across the South, masked and hooded vigilantes whipped, beat, shot, stabbed, and lynched not only African Americans but also Union sympathizers, Republicans, and northern teachers who'd relocated to southern states. In Laurens, long considered a hotbed of Klan activity, tensions devolved into a full-scale riot on the courthouse square, leaving anywhere from seven to fifteen people dead. Only after congressional intervention and passage of the Enforcement Acts—informally known as the Ku Klux Klan Acts, which outlawed mask-wearing and night-riding—did things begin to calm down. In 1871, Laurens became one of nine South Carolina counties to be placed under martial law by President Grant. Thousands of Klansmen were indicted, hundreds were found guilty (though only about sixty-five were imprisoned). By the mid-1870s, the Klan as an organization was more or less dead.

---

were exaggerated or outright fabricated, constructed after the fact by Klan members or sympathizers as propaganda. Parsons points out the relative "shakiness" of the few available contemporary sources describing the event, and contends that the Klan did not expand much beyond Pulaski until the spring of 1868, a year after the purported Nashville meeting. She writes, too, that the growth of the Klan was not organic but rather spurred along by the national media. Newspaper accounts about a "secret" and "outlandish" and "mysterious" organization contributed to the group's growing popularity and mythology; the more the Klan was written about in the press, the more white southerners decided to form their own Ku Klux groups.

Its legacy, however, was anything *but* dead. In fact, as the southern states emerged from Reconstruction, much of the Klan's political agenda was enshrined in law. African Americans were stripped of the vote with the advent of poll taxes, property requirements, and literacy tests. Jim Crow laws cemented their status as second-class citizens. Spectacle or "terror" lynchings—attended by thousands, photographed and viewed by thousands more—peaked in the decades immediately before and after the turn of the century. It was in this context that the KKK re-emerged, this time as a sprawling national movement. In the 1920s, the Klan's second iteration adopted a much more wholesome public image by organizing parades and picnics, sponsoring sports teams and beauty pageants, forming ladies' auxiliaries, even performing a fair amount of charitable work. It was still a white supremacist organization, to be sure, just one dressed up in a prettier, more "patriotic" package.

It was also by far the most popular. At its height, the second Klan swelled to anywhere between four million and six million members, roughly fifty thousand of whom proudly paraded down Pennsylvania Avenue in Washington, D.C., in the summer of 1925. Whereas the old Klan had done much of its work in secret, this new Klan—made up of doctors and lawyers, ministers and business owners, and scores of elected officials, from city councilmen to U.S. senators—didn't have to hide. They wore their hoods, but not their masks. In a mainstream movement, after all, there's no reason to conceal one's identity.

The rebirth had come a decade earlier, in 1915, when a traveling Methodist minister, William Joseph Simmons, decided to resurrect the old order at Stone Mountain, a large geological rock formation (later the site of an enormous bas-relief carving, a paean to the Confederate "heroes" Lee, Jackson, and Davis) on

Thanksgiving night. History regards Simmons as something of a "compulsive joiner," a member of more than a dozen clubs and societies and churches, but a man who nonetheless dreamed of one day founding his own fraternal order. Inspiration struck with the debut of D. W. Griffith's epic three-hour silent film *The Birth of a Nation.* Widely regarded as Hollywood's first official blockbuster, *Birth,* which dramatized the end of the Civil War and the Reconstruction Era, was both a stunning technical achievement and an alarming work of revisionist history. In Griffith's hands, Klansmen were romanticized as noble and heroic. African Americans, largely portrayed by white men in blackface, were depicted as heathens who preyed on white women. The film's glorification of the antebellum era—a dreamscape of Spanish moss and sprawling plantations—sparked a powerful nostalgia. And for Simmons, the phenomenal success of the film—the "greatest picture ever made," according to a *Los Angeles Times* review—presented an opportunity. He began taking out advertisements in various Atlanta newspapers, urging Georgians to join his new Invisible Empire, Knights of the Ku Klux Klan, a "high class order for men of intelligence and character." He brought a small group of followers to the Atlanta premiere of *Birth,* dressed in full robes and pointy white hoods, and brought the Klan back to life by staging a grand tableau: atop Stone Mountain, he constructed an altar (upon which he placed an American flag, an unsheathed sword, and a copy of the Bible) and set fire to an enormous wooden cross.

Despite the theatrics, the second Klan didn't attract a whole lot of members in its first five years. In the spring of 1920, however, Simmons teamed up with a pair of publicists—Edward Young Clarke and Mary Elizabeth "Bessie" Tyler—who launched a massive nationwide recruiting drive. They marketed the Klan as a "100-percent American" organization, pocketing the bulk of each new member's $10 initiation fee. It worked. Membership swelled to more than a hundred thousand within months.

If the fuel for the first Klan had been the tumult and turmoil of Reconstruction, the second Klan found purchase by exploiting white native-born Americans' fears and anxieties in the wake of the First World War, when a global recession, expanding rights for women, the migration of African Americans out of the South, and a flood of European immigrants seemed no less than existential threats to the nation. Second-wave Klansmen longed for a return to "traditional" values and thus rejected anything "foreign"—they were viciously anti-black, anti-Catholic, anti-Semitic, and anti-immigrant. They also co-opted quite a bit of Christian iconography. The ceremonial lighting of the cross dates back to this period, and members were expected (paradoxically) to attend church regularly and to exhibit superior moral character by abstaining from alcohol, premarital sex, adultery, and liberal politics.

Of course, the rise of the second Klan was not without violence. In Alabama, a divorcée was beaten for the "crime" of remarrying. In Oklahoma, "immoral" young women were lashed for riding around in cars with boys. In Louisiana, two white men—detractors of the Klan—were kidnapped, tortured, and decapitated. The breadth and severity of the violence were obscured, however, by the Klan's rebranding of itself as a group of civic-minded cultural warriors. Bigotry became synonymous with patriotism. Harassment and intimidation were normalized. In fact, when the *New York World* ran a lengthy exposé in the fall of 1921—unveiling the Klan's secret rites and rituals, the massive fortunes being amassed by imperial leaders, and less-than-virtuous behavior from its highest-ranking members (Clarke and Tyler, it turned out, had once been arrested at a "house of ill repute")—the publicity only served to make the Klan *more* popular.

Almost as quickly as it had risen to power, however, the Invisible Empire began to fall apart. Members who'd been drawn to the Klan for civic and social reasons started to flee as increasingly gruesome acts of violence were uncovered. After Simmons was ousted from his role as Imperial Wizard and replaced by a dentist named Hiram Evans, the two went to war in the press. By the early 1920s, there was plenty to fight over: the Klan's moneymaking dues apparatus and its real estate portfolio (including an elaborate headquarters in Atlanta, dubbed the Imperial Palace) were by then worth millions. Amid the legal wrangling, a group of Klansmen from Pennsylvania broke away from the national leadership but continued to use the name Ku Klux Klan. Evans promptly sued them for $100,000. Each new lawsuit or court battle exposed still more hypocrisy, corruption, and misdeeds. And it was those two things—money and infighting—that would become staples of the modern Ku Klux Klan's culture.

The third iteration of the KKK—again sparked by sweeping social change, in this case the emerging civil rights movement and the repeal of Jim Crow laws—was always a divided enterprise, a conglomeration of rival groups led by competing rulers. Despite the factionalism, the Klan had by the mid-1960s swelled to levels not seen since the Simmons era. To combat growing vigilante and mob violence, the government stepped in once again. The FBI expanded its notorious COINTELPRO surveillance program, infiltrated Klan factions, and facilitated the HUAC hearings. By the early 1970s, nationwide membership dropped to little more than fifteen hundred. Yet the counter-intelligence operation, though in many ways successful, was not without consequence: the Klan turned suspicious, conspiracy-prone, and vehemently anti-government. To avoid toppling entire organizations, some high-ranking members began to advocate for "lone wolf" terrorism—acts of violence committed by "un-affiliated" individuals or small cells, which could not be traced back to the leadership.

Never again would the KKK enjoy mainstream appeal or widespread political support. But this smaller, more isolated, more marginalized Klan was in many ways less predictable than its predecessors, and potentially more dangerous.

If it was more action he wanted, since the United Klans hadn't been "doing anything," John Howard didn't have to wait long. Robert Scoggin, Grand Dragon of the newly formed Invisible Empire, Knights of the Ku Klux Klan, Realm of South Carolina, was charismatic and gregarious and turned out to be a rabid or-ganizer. "He can sit here an' convince you that he's got a million people in South Car'liner ready to overthrow the United States government, an' you'd believe him," Howard explained to Sims. "Somehow or 'nother the Lord's blessed the man with a gold or silver tongue—either which way you wanta call it—and he can handle people."

Indeed, by the grace of his silver tongue, Scoggin man-aged to win back some of his followers who'd defected after the HUAC hearings. Membership grew further after he orga-nized a slew of rallies across the state. Over the decades, these gatherings had come to resemble a kind of dystopian county fair: Klansmen young and old would assemble in cornfields or cow pastures. Their wives and girlfriends doled out hamburgers and hot dogs from concession stands, while leaders unboxed T-shirts, hats, pins, KKK-branded Bibles, and white supremacist literature. (At a Klan rally, something is always for sale.) Scoggin and his colleagues would then take to the stage—usually a flatbed trailer—and deliver fiery speeches about the evils of welfare, the laziness of blacks, the glory of God, and the coming race war. The festivities concluded, always, with a ceremonial lighting of the cross.

Despite the tenor of the speeches, most rallies functioned as recruiting events, often open to the public and to reporters; they were not typically held in order to plan or commit violence. In the fall of 1970, however, at a rally in Sumter, things went awry. Several members of the UKA (Scoggin's former and now rival outfit) showed up uninvited, and one of the infiltrators was caught trying to sneak in a tape recorder. A scuffle broke out. When it was over, a fifty-year-old grocery store owner named Willie Odom was dead.

"All I knowed about it," Howard told Sims in the fall of 1976, "a guy got killed up the road. A bullet went in up here"—Howard pointed to his head—"and come out here. Killed him instantly."

However little he knew about it, Sims reported that Howard was arrested and indicted along with Scoggin and a half dozen other Klansmen. The charges included malicious mischief, conspiracy to commit robbery, and accessory before and after the fact of murder—but the case was later dropped for lack of evidence.

If Howard's brush with the law rattled him, it certainly didn't affect his membership in the Klan. On the contrary, he began to rise through the ranks. By the fall of 1971, he was calling himself a Grand Titan, Klan parlance for the head of a county or province. And he took his public-facing leadership role seriously. When a high school English teacher from Laurens, Anne Thomson Sheppard, wrote a guest editorial for the *Greenville News* lamenting her fear of the Klan, Howard responded publicly by writing a letter to the editor. He claimed that the Knights of the Ku Klux Klan was a fraternal order rather than a "klandescinal" organization, and denied that Klansmen had ever made threats in Laurens or in any other county in the state. "I say this," Howard wrote, "to tell some misinformed people that this is not the old Ku Klux Klan."

Howard's distinction between the old Klan and the new— between the terrorism of the 1860s and the seemingly benign fraternalism of the 1920s—is one that gets trotted out often, and like all good propaganda, at its core lies a kernel of truth. It's why modern Klansmen routinely claim they aren't racist or anti-black, but rather "pro-white." It's why they reject the label "white supremacist" in favor of "white separatist" or "alt-right." Whatever label one chooses, though, Howard's claim that no Klansman had ever made threats in South Carolina is demonstrably untrue. The vicious assault on future congressman John Lewis by a Rock Hill, South Carolina, Klansman in the spring of 1961, for example, is merely one of the most famous instances.

In any case, it wasn't violence that ultimately drove Howard away from Scoggin. It was, as it almost always is where the Klan is concerned, money and infighting. In her 1978 book, Sims reported that Scoggin earned the nickname "Prophet for Profit" for his enthusiastic hawking of Klan paraphernalia: bumper stickers, autographed photos of Klan dignitaries. (At a rally in Greenville, he once auctioned off "the glass eye of the former Grand Dragon of Pennsylvania." It fetched five dollars.) He developed a reputation as a teller of tales, one prone to stretching the truth. Rumors swirled that Scoggin might have turned government informer. When asked about his leadership style, Howard told Sims: "I seen so much mismanagement, mistreatment of Klanspeople—and too much drinkin." So, sometime between 1971 and 1974, when the drinking and mismanagement got to be too much, Howard switched allegiance again, this time to the National Knights of the Ku Klux Klan under the command of Imperial Wizard James Venable.

An attorney and second-generation Klansman, Venable had his own long and winding history with the hooded order. His uncles had actually owned Stone Mountain and granted the Klan an easement to hold rallies there in the early 1920s. His bigotry, hardened over the decades, was vicious and virulent: he believed that African Americans were "animalistic" in nature, germ-carriers in possession of "inferior" blood. When Martin Luther King Jr. was killed, he suggested the assassin had merely done the world a favor, telling Sims that King was "the worst troublemaker . . . the world's ever known, and yet they honor him as the great emancipator of the nigger race." After breaking away from the United Klans in the mid-1960s, Venable became Shelton's main rival, with aspirations of one day uniting all the Klans under his sole leadership. His National Knights never amassed the size and strength of the UKA, however. By the early 1970s, his following had dwindled to no more than a few hundred.

Ironically, that may have proved a boon to John Howard. The Klan's power structure mimics a representative democracy, with a central, national figure—the Imperial Wizard—propped up by state, regional, and local leaders, all of whom are (ostensibly) elected to office. It's certainly easier to rise through the ranks of a smaller organization, and it wasn't long before Howard was elevated again, to the rank of Grand Dragon. As a statewide leader, Howard would be responsible for setting up new klaverns, organizing rallies, and driving recruitment. In the summer of 1975, with his authority and influence on the rise, he descended on the small town of Greenwood, not long after a white highway patrolman shot and killed a young black man. A local chapter of the NAACP had petitioned for the cop's suspension and sponsored a protest march, which the Klan intended to counterprotest.

It turned out to be something of an odd reunion: representatives of Shelton's UKA were there, steering a twelve-car motorcade through the streets of downtown Greenwood. Across town, Scoggin presided over a rally attended by some fifteen hundred Klansmen. Howard's rally, on the other hand, turned out to be little more than a few National Knights waving hand-lettered signs—WE SUPPORT LAW AND ORDER!—on the side of the road for a few hours.

It's impossible to know if Howard was bothered by the weak showing. (He'd anticipated as many as four hundred protesters.) But just one month later, in September 1975, he broke ranks again. Whether by choice or by sheer necessity, though, is a little harder to parse. According to Venable, Howard—along with four other Grand Dragons—had attended a secret meeting, at which he violated his oath as a Klansman by participating in an "illegal election," and had therefore been banished forever. According to Howard and his co-conspirators, Venable was old and senile, and they'd willingly split from the National Knights.

"Our dream is to one day overcome all this jealousy an' bickerin an' power struggles an' money-grabbin and unite into one," Howard explained to Sims in the spring of 1976. But no matter how many factions he joined, the bickering and money-grabbing never ceased. Virtually all of the leaders he'd once stood behind were felled by their own greed, pride, or hubris.

Scoggin, the Prophet for Profit, grew ever more eccentric over the years, his influence gradually waning until he ceased being active sometime in the early 1980s. In 1987, Robert Shelton and his UKA were sued into bankruptcy by the Southern Poverty Law Center, after two of Shelton's acolytes lynched a black teenager in Mobile, Alabama. Venable's outfit never recovered from the defection of Howard and the other Grand Dragons; he died in a nursing home in 1993, suffering from Alzheimer's, cancer, and pneumonia.

Howard continued to bounce from one Klan faction to the next, all the way through to the early 1990s. Most of these factions were small and floundering, and many of them fell apart not long after Howard pledged his membership. Upon each sect's demise, he would carry with him a cadre of core followers—perhaps as few as twenty members, perhaps many more—and link up with some new organization.

Then, sometime in 1993 or 1994, he finally decided to start his own group—in partnership with a Pennsylvania-based Grand Dragon.

It's difficult to determine when, exactly, Howard first met Barry Black. Harder still is determining why Howard had any faith in Black's ability to help unite the Klans, or to avoid the fate of every other Imperial Wizard to whom he'd once been loyal. Howard had largely managed to avoid any trouble with the law; Black, on the other hand, had a lengthy criminal record, with convictions for larceny, burglary, and a firearms violation. He had escaped from police custody twice—once from the Greene County Jail outside Pittsburgh, and later from a psychiatric unit at Washington Hospital, where he'd been sent for evaluation. Black was a large man, bald, with a thick neck, broad shoulders, and a worldview the Southern Poverty Law Center deemed "emblematic of the gutter aspects" of the Klan.

What Black reportedly had was followers, hundreds of them, in as many as seven states. So Howard and Black ultimately decided to merge their factions.

For a supposedly "secret" order, the Ku Klux Klan often has a very public face. Though some factions are extremely clandestine, others function not entirely unlike legitimate businesses—which is to say they are legally incorporated entities, with a paper trail and a tax status. According to paperwork filed with the South Carolina secretary of state, Howard and Black's new entity—the Keystone Knights of the Ku Klux Klan—would be incorporated as a religious nonprofit; its mission was to protect "the patriot beliefs in Christ" and "Ango [*sic*] Saxon Heritage." Howard and Black referred to themselves as "reverends," and as vice president and president, respectively, in their Articles of Incorporation. The group's principal office, its primary place of business, was listed as 108 W. Laurens Street—the old Echo theater.

Howard had quietly purchased the building back in 1992, for the bargain price of $4,000. Even then, he had designs on one day turning the place into a meeting hall and a Klan museum, funded by some sort of retail shop. Everything he had learned about the Klan had been passed down to him via older members; anything the Klan might accomplish in the future would be at the hands of a new generation. A Klan museum, in addition to a moneymaking enterprise, was about legitimacy and posterity—things Howard cared about deeply. Because by then, at forty-seven years old, with his career as a Klansman entering the phase when a man starts considering his legacy, he had something better than a fancy-sounding title or a source of income. He'd found a protégé.

three

THE PERFECT RECRUIT

By the time a young man named Michael Burden turned up in Laurens at the tail end of 1989, John Howard had been a Klansman for half his life. He was remarried by then, to a round, doughy woman with a mop of short brown curls, Hazel. His kids were grown. And for the better part of a decade, he'd been living on a secluded plot of land just off Highway 221, right on the border of Laurens and Spartanburg Counties, in the small town of Lanford.

Although "town" is a bit of a stretch. Lanford doesn't even show up on most maps of the area; it's little more than a deserted railroad community, a ghost town dotted with a few falling-down, turn-of-the-century structures that seem to sink deeper into the brush with each passing year. Howard's property, eight-tenths of an acre bounded to the east by the old C&WC railway, was likewise overgrown and unkempt; rising from patches of gravel and thickets of scratchgrass were a dilapidated two-story frame house—white, with a rust-colored roof—two mobile homes, and a tin shack, out of which he operated his business, Plantation Concrete.

Since the Klan's rebirth at Stone Mountain in 1915, high-ranking leaders have often tried to eke out a living on the backs of their members, usually by cobbling together a nominal salary (subsidized by membership dues) and hawking white supremacist and KKK-branded merchandise. Some of the more industrious have managed to live far beyond the means of their followers. Bessie Tyler, one-half of the publicity duo that transformed William Joseph Simmons's struggling fraternal club into a national movement, built a palatial residence on fourteen acres of land in Buckhead, a ritzy section of uptown Atlanta. The UKA's Bob Jones, a lightning rod salesman by day, very famously drove around in a shiny new Cadillac, which was gifted to him by fellow Klansmen in the winter of 1964.

John Howard never amassed that sort of wealth. Like most of the piedmont's working poor, he'd taken a job in the mills as a young man. By the mid-1970s, as Howard entered his thirties and was elevated to the rank of Grand Dragon, he was still making little more than minimum wage working as an orderly at the Whitten Center, a state-run facility for disabled adults and children. As the decades rolled by and Howard's health declined, his primary source of income became the family business. Privately, some Laurens natives have described Plantation Concrete as little more than a front for the Klan, but by all accounts Howard did manage to sell some stuff: cement birdbaths, fountains, planters, and other forms of "ornamental concrete." For those who shared his political persuasions, he also offered a range of more colorful items, from cement skulls to miniature Klansman statues.

Exactly what Mike Burden was doing walking through such a desolate area isn't entirely clear—most details of his upbringing aren't, and to this day he isn't particularly forthcoming. But the gist of the story, the story Burden tells when he is compelled to talk about his background, is that he got caught in a storm one afternoon, saw a light on in Howard's shop, and asked if he might set down for a bit to get out of the rain. The details vary. In interviews with the *Los Angeles Times*, Burden claimed to have met Howard three years earlier, in 1986, shortly after he was kicked out of high school. In some versions of the story, he portrays himself as essentially homeless, sleeping most nights in an abandoned car. In other versions, he was living in a friend's vehicle. Mike Burden has trouble with details. But the basic outline of the story remains the same: the men introduced themselves, and Howard's face suddenly brightened with recognition. Apparently he and Burden's parents had long ago been part of the same "organization."

"He told me, 'Son, I've held you when you was a baby and changed your diapers!'"

The coincidence struck Burden as unlikely. "You're full of crap," he said.

"No," Howard shot back. "*You* were."

Burden was a few months shy of twenty years old, thin and wiry—five foot eleven, 147 pounds—with an edginess about him. He was cagey, drawn in on himself. His brown hair, shaggy and unkempt, was usually shoved under a backward ball cap, and he held his narrow jaw in such a way that his bottom teeth—straight, if tobacco-stained—were more readily visible than his upper incisors.

By that time, Howard's property in Lanford had become a crash pad of sorts for a revolving cast of veteran Klansmen. His second-born son, Dwayne, was in his early twenties and more or less living at home. Howard's longtime friend and associate Charles Murphy made frequent appearances, popping over from the nearby town of Woodruff to attend meetings or strategy sessions. At some point, a rail-thin bespectacled Klansman in his late fifties, William Hoff—known to his friends as "Wild Bill"—just sort of showed up and never left.

In addition to the various old-timers stopping by or taking up residence, there was often a slew of youngsters running around, as Plantation Concrete was more or less operated by teenagers. (Kids of fellow Klansmen, mostly, sent up to Lanford by their parents—ostensibly to learn the value of a hard day's work.) By the time the rain stopped on that first day, Howard had offered Burden a job, too. Instead of cash, however, the young man would be paid in kind: food to eat, clothes to wear, a roof over his head. For the next seven years, Burden's primary place of residence would be a single-wide trailer on the edge of the Lanford property.

The Klan, like other white supremacist organizations, has a long history of pursuing young men and boys for recruitment—papering high school parking lots with racist literature, staking out concert halls and music venues, and infiltrating college campuses are all popular tactics. Disaffected young men and boys, in particular, make for especially prime targets. Bill Riccio, an Alabama-based neo-Nazi who rose to power in the late 1980s, readily admitted that he would comb local shopping malls and swimming pools in search of kids to lure back to his Birmingham-area headquarters. In interviews with the Southern Poverty Law Center's *Intelligence Report*, a victim of Riccio's alleged sex abuse put it more succinctly: "He would prey on kids with legal problems, emotional problems, and disadvantaged kids."

There's no evidence that John Howard actively sought out disadvantaged youth for *his* klavern, but Michael Burden certainly would've fit the profile. His biological parents divorced when he was five, and his father—again, for reasons that aren't entirely clear—promptly severed all contact. "His exact words," Burden says, "were, 'I don't want that little bastard around anymore.'" Burden's mother soon took up with a new man, a welder, setting off a nomadic ten years during which the trio bounced from oil town to oil town across the Southwest. It was not a happy childhood. And in the way of male role models, Burden's stepfather wasn't much of an improvement over the one who'd split. He was, according to Burden, a drunk with a penchant for blowing his paycheck at the local watering hole rather than on, say, food for the family. By the time he turned sixteen, Burden had left—and wound up right back where he had started: in Laurens.

THE MISEDUCATION OF Mike Burden began virtually the moment he stepped foot on Howard's property. Though his days were suddenly taken up with work related to the concrete business—accepting and filling orders, mixing cement, maintaining and repairing machinery—his evenings were largely free for socializing. Talk invariably turned to the Klan, a topic on which John Howard seemed to be a fount of wisdom.

The Anti-Defamation League once wrote of the UKA's leader, Robert Shelton: "He has no hobbies, does not indulge in sports, and has no other interests" beyond the KKK. Howard's identity, too, was bound up in being a Klansman. The ring he wore, which resembled a class ring with a red stone in the center, featured an embossed *A*—shorthand for "AKIA," a 1920s-era password meaning "A Klansman I Am." On the wall of his living room was a studio portrait, taken back in the mid-1970s, featuring a younger, thinner Howard in full Klan regalia. The second floor of his crumbling farmhouse had been turned into a meeting hall, appointed with several rows of folding chairs and a makeshift podium. Along the walls were framed snapshots of Howard cavorting with other state-level leaders of the KKK, as well as old black-and-white and sepia-tone prints of notable Klansmen throughout history: members gathered at the Imperial Palace back in the 1920s, a parade of Klansmen marching through the streets of Washington, D.C., headshots of William Joseph Simmons and Hiram Evans.

Ninety percent of what he had heard about the Klan, Howard assured Burden, was not the truth. He peddled a version of history—lifted almost verbatim from *The Birth of a Nation*—that painted the Reconstruction-era Klan as a necessity, a force for good in the otherwise devastated southern states. Burden eagerly lapped up the tenets of Lost Cause mythology: the belief that the Civil War was not about slavery; that northerners, intent on punishing the rebels for secession, had set out to destroy their way of life. Howard even offered proof that the Klan "wasn't racist," in the form of an old photograph of black Confederate soldiers in full battle dress, muskets at their sides, ready to march on behalf of the South.

When it came to the legacy of William Joseph Simmons and his "fraternal" Klan, Howard's lectures took on a practically evangelical pitch. "He seen a vision in the sky when he was a young man," Howard said matter-of-factly. (Simmons long claimed to have been inspired by a late-night vision of men on horseback, galloping across the horizon.) "*God* gave him a vision to create the Knights of the Ku Klux Klan." How else could he have built a million-man movement from nothing? Howard regularly ticked off the names of great men—presidents, senators, governors—who had been members, and lamented that history was being "cleaned up" to erase their legacy. He made the Klan sound like a noble cause. It wasn't long before Burden wanted to join—indeed, developed a kind of obsession. "I ate, slept, drank, and studied the Klan," he told *The State*, a Columbia newspaper.

Under Howard's tutelage, Burden became something of an expert in the Klan's culture and history, or what's referred to as "Klancraft." He learned the pledges and oaths, as well as the ranks and titles of the various officers, from the Exalted Cyclops (the head of a klavern) to the Klaliff (vice president of a klavern) and the Kludd (or chaplain), who presides over weddings and funerals. He was taught how to light the cross, a ceremony that Klansmen insist is not in any way meant to be sacrilegious but is rather a symbol of their devotion and Christian faith. Burden also learned the significance of the Mystic Insignia of a Klansman (MIOAK), the red-and-white patch worn over the left breast on their traditional robes. "It looks like a cross from a distance, but if you look real close, you'll see a little square in the middle of it," Burden says. Place a piece of paper or your thumb over that square, and the "cross" becomes four *K*'s, representing the Knights of the Ku Klux Klan. In the center of the patch is a red swirl, which Klansmen refer to as a blood drop, meant to represent the blood of Christ, the "purity" of Christ, or the blood to be shed in defense of the white race.

What Burden did not know, not for a long time, is that virtually every rite and ritual he learned was a contemporary reinterpretation, a cynical attempt to make the modern Klan seem more legitimate and more palatable. The MIOAK, for example, is a relic of the Simmons era, but the "blood drop" was not originally intended to represent blood, and certainly not Christ's.

It was one half of a yin-yang symbol featuring the dates 1866 and 1915 (representing the first and second Klans, respectively). Since the white half of the symbol didn't show up well against the white background of the patch, however, it was eventually dropped, leaving a lone red swirl. Klansmen didn't start calling the swirl a blood drop until the 1960s and '70s, after the HUAC hearings had decimated their membership.

The cross burning, meanwhile, was merely a case of life imitating art: *The Birth of a Nation* depicted Klansmen setting crosses ablaze because director D. W. Griffith liked the visual. William Joseph Simmons then borrowed the visual when he revived the Klan at Stone Mountain. Perhaps the most famous of the Klan's rites and ceremonies was no more than an invention of Hollywood.

As for Howard's Civil War–era photograph depicting black Confederate soldiers—his "proof" that the Klan wasn't racist—it was fake. The photo, a doctored image of black *Union* soldiers, has circulated among neo-Confederates and members of the far right for decades.

Despite John Howard's influence and tutelage, Burden's first real brush with the hooded order at large, beyond the relatively limited interactions he'd had at Plantation Concrete, did not go the way he'd imagined. Upon arriving at an inter-Klan rally on Stone Mountain sometime in 1990 or 1991, he was surprised to find the place overrun by neo-Nazis.

In the world of white supremacy, the Ku Klux Klan, neo-Nazis, and skinheads represent three distinct movements, each with its own dogma and doctrine. After the HUAC hearings and COINTELPRO investigations, however, these groups began to merge and coalesce, sharing a suspicion of centralized government and a mutual sense of victimization and persecution. By the time Mike Burden joined up, it wasn't unusual to find Third Reich symbolism—swastikas, the double-*sig* rune of Hitler's SS—at a Klan event, nor was it unheard-of to see robed Klansmen chatting it up with kids in Dr. Martens and suspenders. Yet Burden was prepared for none of that. He'd been reared on the gospel of William Joseph Simmons, but the skinheads cavorting around Stone Mountain were "all about 'Sieg Heil' and all that stuff," he says, "and I was like *hell no*. That ain't even American!"

Feeling out of his depth and on edge, Burden proceeded to get into an argument with a Grand Dragon from the UKA, an exceedingly short man—no more than five foot four—with an outsized ego Burden found profoundly irritating. He wound up getting kicked out of the rally.

Next up was an event in North Carolina, this one organized by James Farrands of the Invisible Empire (yet another splinter group, not to be confused with Simmons's or Scoggin's earlier movements). Something about that rally made Burden feel more at home. Farrands had taken to calling himself a "new breed" of Klansman. He insisted that he wasn't violent and didn't "hate" anybody. Within a few years' time he would banish neo-Nazis and skinheads in an attempt to rehabilitate the Klan's image.

Of course, even in those days Burden could acknowledge the Klan's legacy of violence. "There's not a lot of good history," he admits. "For every positive thing I found, ten negatives took its place. I mean, you got the massacre in Greensboro. . . ."

The Greensboro Massacre was the November 1979 climax of long-simmering tension between the Klan and members of the Communist Workers Party, which had been organizing black textile workers in small towns across the state. On November 3, the CWP staged a "Death to the Klan" rally at Morningside Homes, a predominantly black housing project. Shortly before 11:30 a.m., a half hour before the rally was set to begin, a nine-car caravan of Klansmen and members of the American Nazi Party drove past the throngs of assembling protesters. Some of the demonstrators began to beat on the vehicles, and within seconds the confrontation devolved into a shootout. Five members of the CWP were left dead.

In the aftermath, a number of Klan factions across the Carolinas went dark. Howard watched as membership in his group plummeted to just forty. Starting in the summer of 1985, however, the hooded order began to make a very public resurgence, in part by requesting parade permits from city councils in the South Carolina towns of Blacksburg, Clinton, and Laurens. In interviews with the press, Howard's longtime friend Charles Murphy announced plans to march in still more cities, attributing the sudden increase in visibility to new and "better" leadership. He was referring to a man named Horace King, Grand Dragon of the newly formed Christian Knights, who reported to a man named Virgil Griffin—one of the architects of the massacre in Greensboro.

Public authorities had by then grown skeptical of the Klan's actual reach and influence. The chief of the South Carolina State Law Enforcement Division insisted to the *Greenville News* that folks were "getting too smart" to join. "People are just not going to support [the Klan]. This is 1985," he said. And for a time it seemed as though he might have been right. Only a handful of marchers showed up in Blacksburg, and officials in Clinton chose to deny the Klan a permit after receiving a slew of irate and threatening phone calls. The city of Laurens quickly followed suit, denying a permit on the grounds that violence and lawlessness were likely. "We had Greensboro on our minds," Mayor Dominick said, explaining the decision to reporters.

The denials, however, had an unintended consequence: they triggered a wave of First Amendment lawsuits, all of which the Klan won. After that, the Christian Knights organized marches in Gaffney, Spartanburg, Fountain Inn, Mauldin, Woodruff, Greer, Greenville, and Anderson. In 1987, they hit Summerville and Charleston. In 1988, they rallied in Greenwood and Newberry. In the summer of 1990—the same week that Rev. Kennedy got into a public spat with the mayor in the wake of Bobo Cook's death—the Klan obtained a permit to counterprotest.

It's not clear if John Howard ever officially joined the Christian Knights, but by the early 1990s, his Keystone Klan and Horace King's outfit had become the two largest factions in the state.

As THE MONTHS and then years slipped by, Howard and Burden developed a bond that, to outsiders, seemed an awful lot like a father-son relationship. (Not that it didn't produce complications. Howard's son Dwayne was a fellow Klansman, and his relationship with Burden—a mere three years his junior— slowly evolved from a friendship into a rivalry, and finally into a sometimes volatile dynamic fraught with jealousy and tension.) Upon closer inspection, however, Burden's role at the Lanford house, in the Klan, and within Howard's inner circle might have been less like that of a son and more like that of a soldier. "He could ask me anything," Burden said. "He could wake me up in the middle of the night. He could tell me, 'Go out there, set down and wait on somebody to deliver a load of concrete at two o'clock in the morning.' I'd get up, no questions asked. No arguments or nuthin. Just get up and go do it."

For his loyalty, Burden was rewarded. Sometime after John Howard and Barry Black merged their organizations in the early 1990s, Burden was made an Emperor's Night-Hawk—in other words, head of Klan security. At rallies, he and a team of subordinates monitored the perimeter of the field or pasture, patrolled the parking lot, patted people down in search of contraband. "My unit actually had a wand," he said. "We wanded you down for firearms or anything like that." At the same time, he began to stockpile weapons—pistols, shotguns, an SKS semi-automatic rifle, a .30-.30 rifle with a two-hundred-yard scope—and acquire books on explosives: *The Poor Man's James Bond, The Anarchist Cookbook*. When Howard met with other high-level leaders—Barry Black, Charles Murphy, Virgil Griffin, Horace King—Burden assumed the role of bodyguard.

The Klan has always been performative in nature. The hoods and robes, the cross-burning, the secrecy of the order itself—the theatrical elements—are in many ways just as intimidating (and effective) as the commission of violence. But as much as they perform for their victims, Klansmen perform for each other, too. Back in the early 1960s, for example, when the Klan was perhaps more fractured than at any other time in its history, the heads of various splinter groups met in Indian Springs, Georgia, to discuss a merger. Robert Shelton, then heading up a small Alabama-based faction, arrived with an eight-man security detail dressed in paramilitary garb. It was a performance—a show of strength—and it worked. By meeting's end, Shelton had been named Imperial Wizard of the new UKA.

Performing—acting out the role of enforcer—made Burden feel powerful, too, as did his sudden proximity to so many leaders within the movement. He reveled in their stories of long-ago bombings and night rides. He emulated their tough talk and bravado.

But nobody could spin a yarn quite like "Wild Bill" Hoff.

A New York native, Hoff had arrived at a rally in North Carolina in the early 1990s, where he met and befriended John Howard. Several weeks later he turned up in Lanford, towing a U-Haul. "He came down supposedly to visit," Burden says, "but he blew the engine in his car pullin his trailer." Hoff's "visit," extended little by little relative to his car trouble, gradually evolved into a permanent trip. Nobody seemed to have the heart to tell him he'd perhaps overstayed his welcome. "It's kinda hard to tell a sixty-year-old man, 'You got to go.'"

Indeed, there was a fragility about Wild Bill—he was of slight build, hardly 150 pounds, with a receding hairline and Coke-bottle glasses. The moniker, however, was completely in line with the stories he told about himself, elaborate fictions meant to cultivate the image of a larger-than-life persona. Hoff told his fellow Klansmen that he'd served as a mercenary in Angola and Rhodesia; that he'd once mounted a run for Senate in the state of New York (and garnered an astonishing *seventy thousand* write-in votes); that his parents had been sent to a detention camp during World War II for being Nazi sympathizers; that while he was growing up, his mother would read selections from Hitler's *Mein Kampf* to the children each night.

None of it was true. The real story of Hoff's life, however, is just as wild—and far more tragic.

William Hoff wasn't raised to hate. He'd grown up in the heavily mixed ghettoes of South Brooklyn in the 1930s and '40s, where he was exposed to—and appreciated—a variety of customs and cultures. He played basketball with black and Latino kids from the neighborhood, learned snippets of Italian from the wannabe mobsters and Yiddish from the Jewish immigrants. But then he dropped out of high school, enlisted in the navy, and got himself dishonorably discharged after a violent altercation with a black sailor. After that, things for Wild Bill fell apart. In the 1960s, during the same period when his brother Donald became a Methodist minister and a member of the NAACP, Bill turned to political extremism, joining up with the American Nazi Party, the States Rights Party, and the Ku Klux Klan. In 1968, he was arrested in New York City for plotting to blow up a roomful of "active leftists" and draft resistors. His family was baffled. "I never knew Billy to be anti-Negro, anti-Jew, or anti-anything until he came out of the Navy," Donald explained to the Elmira *Star-Gazette* in a 1969 interview. "I think he found something that gave foundation to his fear and confusion, his sense of injustice."

Hoff ultimately served six years at Attica Correctional Facility. (The rare true detail in his otherwise outrageous stories was the fact that he'd been present for the 1971 Attica riots.) But he rejoined the Klan after his parole ended, rising as high as Grand Dragon in New York. Then, in a truly bizarre twist, he took a job as a receptionist at a black-owned employment agency, Third World Personnel Services, which specialized in helping minorities find jobs. Hoff's coworkers had no knowledge of his criminal history or his ties to the white supremacist movement; on the contrary, they described him as mild-mannered, even avuncular. Hoff fled south only after being outed as a Klansman by the Jewish Defense Organization, a militant outfit with its own history of violence.

Sociologists have long understood that ideology is not always the primary motivation among people who join white supremacist and organized hate movements. "It's not the racist beliefs of groups like the Klan that are so appealing to men like Burden," Jack Levin, director of the Brudnick Center on Violence and Social Conflict at Northeastern University, said in interviews with *The State*. "It's the need to belong, the need to feel important. [Burden] sounds like the perfect recruit." Kathleen Blee, dean of the School of Arts and Sciences at the University of Pittsburgh and the author of three books on organized racism, explained to the *University Times* that most of the Klan members and neo-Nazis she has studied or interviewed over the years were not particularly racist when they joined. "If you met these people when they were getting involved, they wouldn't really strike you as off the charts in their racism," she said. "But once they are in it for a while, that worldview really deepens."

The more Burden slipped into his role of bodyguard, the more stories he absorbed about committing violence with impunity, the more he began to parrot Howard's rhetoric and vitriol, the more committed he became to the cause. "I was led to believe that was family," he later told reporters. "That was my life. That was my destiny. And I done the best I could to live up to it."

BY THE TIME John Howard purchased the old Echo theater, the crime and drug use that so troubled Rev. Kennedy in the mid-1980s had worsened. In the smallest towns, the collapse of the textile industry had proved devastating: the Riegel mill, an eighty-year-old plant in the nearby hamlet of Ware Shoals, laid off 850 workers back in 1982, a figure equivalent to more than one-third of the town's entire population. Two years later, another 900 people were put out of work. As mill after mill across the Upstate shuttered—thirty-one of the region's manufacturing plants closed in 1983 alone—the effects rippled outward. In Iva, roughly forty miles southwest of Laurens, the proprietor of a local restaurant estimated to reporters that nearly half his business had come from mill workers. For municipal governments, the collapse meant a significant loss of tax revenue. In the village of Lockhart, reporters predicted that the closing of the Milliken mill, in 1994, would wind up being a "death bell."

As the county seat, Laurens had fared a little better (Watts Mill was still operational), but not by much. Revenues at the downtown businesses had been dropping for the better part of a decade, amid competition from shopping centers and strip malls out by the highway and the offerings of more prosperous towns, especially Spartanburg and Greenville. Over time, the historic town square had grown more and more deserted. The Echo, in particular, was a shambles. "We walked in there and it was completely rotted," Burden said. "I mean, we had to put in floors, ceilings, walls, everything. We basically rebuilt that thing from the ground up."

From the start, Burden had been on board with Howard's plan to open a Klan museum and some sort of gift shop, and the two spoke often about their shared vision for the space. Exhibits curated from Howard's extensive personal collection would include the very items Burden had found so fascinating as a lost and lonely nineteen-year-old: old photographs, charters, and publications from the Simmons-era Klan, mainly. Somewhere in the rear of the building, out of view from prying eyes and passersby, they would set up a working Klan lodge, turning the old theater into a headquarters for the Keystone Knights. They talked idly about the stir such a store would cause in Laurens, and fantasized about how much money they might make. Beyond that, a shop in the middle of the town square would give them a huge leg up when it came to recruitment.

Renovations began sometime in late 1992 or early 1993 in

what had been the lobby and concessions area, a modest-sized room facing West Laurens Street. The rear of the building, or what had once been the actual screening room—a cavernous space, with thirty-foot ceilings, a sagging floor, and a leaking roof—would require months of labor. The repairs were tedious and slow-going, however, as Howard had neither the money nor the inclination to hire a general contractor; the project was funded in fits and starts, largely from incoming membership dues.

While progress at the store may have been slow, Burden's status within the Klan continued to rise: sometime in 1993 or 1994, he was promoted again, this time to the position of Exalted Cyclops. Burden relished his position as head of the klavern, the sense of power and control it gave him. "If you were in my lodge and I didn't prefer a thing that you said or done," he once explained to a reporter from *The State*, "I'd say, 'Sit down, Klansman. You out of order.'" He loved the ceremony of Klan rituals: gaveling weekly meetings to order, reciting the sacred language of the Klan's 1920s-era rulebook, written by Simmons himself. One of his favorite activities was the initiation of new recruits.

The process, referred to as "naturalization," is considered a sacred ritual, though in truth it bears more resemblance to college fraternity hazing. There are variations from klavern to klavern, but the ceremony centers on proving one's loyalty and trust. To do that, new recruits are typically blindfolded, then they might be placed in a row—each Klansman's hand positioned on the shoulder of the man in front of him—and led through a wooded area or over a patch of rough terrain while being intimidated by sudden shouts and sounds, like the not-so-far-off report of a rifle. Alternatively, they might be ordered to stand stock-still and refrain from flinching while someone pokes or prods them, or startles them with the whirring of a revolver wheel.

"During our initiation," Burden says, "one of the things that we always told 'em was, 'Never tell anybody what the blood drop means'—the blood drop means purity. So during the initiation we're constantly bombardin 'em with the word *purity*. And how significant it is." Burden and his fellow officers would shout rapid-fire questions at their initiates: *Will you be loyal to your oath? Do you pledge to stand up for the white race?* After a while, someone would suddenly ask: *What does the blood drop mean?* And invariably, some poor recruit would call out, "Purity!" When that happened, Burden was there to administer a little shock—a kind of negative-reinforcement therapy, the way one might train a dog with an electric anti-bark collar. Burden, however, used a cattle prod.

"One of the best ones I had—the guy was every bit of 250 pounds. He had twenty-something-inch arms. I mean, this guy was huge. He looked like John Cena. He's standing there with his back to me, and I got this cattle prod, and he shouts 'purity' and as soon as he did I come up between his legs, barely caught him in the middle section between his groin and his butt, and that guy goes 'Yeowwww!' I couldn't handle it. I just busted out laughing. I was rollin on the floor."

If his new recruits had a problem with the prodding, they didn't say much. "Afterwards we'd all get together and we'd cut up and joke and stuff like that. And they'd get to do it next time." Initiation also marked the beginning of a series of payments: the initiation fee itself, plus the procurement of a hood and robe and monthly dues of fifteen or twenty bucks. In a blighted town like Laurens, that kind of financial commitment was no small thing.

. . .

A YEAR OR so into renovations at the Echo, Burden and his team had made enough progress that a portion of the old screening room in the back of the theater could be converted into a makeshift lodge. A temporary wall was erected to split the space in half, and the ceiling above the still-unfinished section was covered with a tarp (repairs on the roof would stretch on for many more months). Howard, meanwhile, signed a lease with his Imperial Wizard, Barry Black—on Keystone Knights letterhead—granting him "full authority" of the lodge for a period of ninety-nine years. Howard would retain exclusive rights to the museum, which would be housed, at first, in the corridor behind the lobby.

With the museum and meeting hall slowly coming together, Howard and Burden decided to focus on the shop at the front of the building, as they would need the proceeds to pay for additional repairs—and there was good reason to think they'd find a market for the sale of Klan memorabilia. Back in 1992, the owners of a 130-year-old farmhouse in Freemont, Michigan, discovered a treasure trove of 1920s-era Klan artifacts. They didn't know what to do with the hoods and robes and letters and faded documents, so they held an auction. They had no way of knowing the event would attract hundreds of curious neighbors as well as serious collectors, or that the total haul from the sale of roughly 250 items would approach $30,000.

Over the coming months, Howard and Burden traveled up and down the East Coast, searching for relics and tokens from that same era: rings, watch fobs, official Klan charters, membership cards. If they couldn't find a particular item, they made it themselves: white bedsheets, for example, could be stitched into an "official" Klan robe—manufactured for next to nothing and sold for more than $100. The rest of the shop's floor space would be filled out with generic "southern pride" knickknacks: Confederate-flag license plates, decals, flip-flops, bathing suits. Then there were the other items: silk-screened T-shirts with the likeness of Martin Luther King Jr. in the crosshairs of a rifle scope, pickaninny figurines. "I think probably the worst thing we actually had in there . . . ," Burden said, thinking. "We made a doorknocker. I had seen an image of it, and I've always done woodwork, so I made a black gingerbread man that screwed to your door. And he was painted with his overalls, painted black. Then you had a Klansman standing there, and I painted the robe and everything. You pull the string at the bottom of it, he'd swing a bat, crack the black guy in the head knockin on the door. That was probably the meanest thing we actually had in there."

The further along they got in the process, the more Howard must have started to sense the potential of his new asset—and perhaps the chaos and controversy he was about to unleash in his own hometown. No doubt he was familiar with a string of recent lawsuits then plaguing Klan groups across the country. (Farrands's Invisible Empire had just been sued into bankruptcy by the Southern Poverty Law Center for pelting protesters with bottles and rocks during a civil rights march; the faction lost the deed to its headquarters as part of the settlement.) So he decided that keeping the shop safe would require a somewhat counterintuitive approach: He'd need to sell it. Or sell *part* of it, at least.

"Life estates" are deeds that split ownership of real property between two (or more) parties: the life tenant, who retains exclusive rights to the property during his or her lifetime, and the remainderman, who takes possession of the property upon the life tenant's death. Life estates are most often used in estate planning—a parent can "give" his or her child the family home, for example, without giving up the right to live in it. In the case of the Redneck Shop, however, Howard had something else in mind. He figured a dual-ownership situation would make it harder for an outside party to somehow wrest control of the shop away from him. "It was his way of protecting it," said Burden. "He wanted to make sure that if something came up, nobody could sue for the shop. He would be able to use it forever."

Howard could have chosen his son Dwayne to be the beneficiary—Dwayne was, after all, a fellow Klansman. But instead he chose Michael Burden.

Signing on to the deed was, for Burden, a total no-brainer: now, no matter what happened in the future, he'd always have the shop to fall back on. It was the first time he'd ever owned what might be described as an asset—it was the first time he'd ever owned *anything*, really. And as the shop's grand opening drew near, Burden realized that he was the most content he had ever been in his life. He'd been plucked from abject poverty and given a sense of purpose, a leadership role in what he thought of as a storied organization. He'd found for himself a new family. There just wasn't much more that he needed—that is, until one afternoon in the winter of 1995, when he encountered something it hadn't even occurred to him to want.

He was up in the rafters at the Echo, repairing some rotted ceiling joists, when he noticed the petite brunette standing some forty feet below. "She had on a pair of little white Daisy Duke shorts," he said later. "Hair down past her shoulders, and this little pink tank top. I just sat there, transfixed. I forgot what I was doin."

Her name—Burden already knew—was Judy.

four

BURN IT DOWN

On a February afternoon not long after his clandestine meeting outside the Beasley Mortuary, Rev. Kennedy steered his car into the crumbling parking lot of Foggie's Barber Shop, housed in a squat white building on a back alley just north of the courthouse square.

"'Bout time you walked in the door, Rev!"

Willie Foggie, the shop's fifty-eight-year-old proprietor, a large man with kind eyes and a shock of white hair, was standing behind one of four salon chairs, clippers in hand, gesturing toward the packed waiting area. "Everybody talkin 'bout the KKK."

Secrets don't stay secret long in a town as tiny as Laurens, and word about a Klan-backed business had already started to trickle out into the community. The barbershop, a thirty-year fixture of the black community, was busier than usual, though perhaps only a third of the patrons were actually there for haircuts. The rest had arrived merely to talk. Foggie's was as much a social club as it was a barbershop. Some of the old-timers could reliably be found there every day, the same time of day, holding court from one of the folding chairs along the back wall. The shop itself was small, made smaller still by piles of clutter: stacks of paperwork, cardboard boxes, two televisions, a coffee machine, razors and clippers and shaving cream canisters and Styrofoam takeout containers. What it lacked in tidiness, however, it made up for in warmth: lining the walls were hundreds of photos of Foggie's friends and family, thumbtacked one atop the other, fighting for space with yellowed newspaper clippings and football pennants and a framed jersey. Foggie's youngest son, Rickey, was something of a hometown hero; he'd led the Laurens Raiders to their first-ever state championship back in 1983.

Foggie, too, was something of an institution, as much therapist as barber. Time seemed to slow down inside his shop. Customers waited patiently even as the clippers stopped clipping and Foggie got swept up in conversation. But that day in mid-February, the vibe was tense.

"You believe this, Rev?" one of the younger patrons called out. "The Klan gonna open a store across from the *courthouse?*"

"I know," Kennedy said, shaking his head. "I've been looking into it for a while."

"When you find out?"

"Someone mentioned something to me about it a while back," Kennedy said.

"Who?"

"A friend."

Kennedy wasn't about to give up the source of his information, but it was true that he had been investigating, meandering past the storefront and trying to peer inside the windows, meeting privately with a few well-placed folks within the community.

It hadn't taken him long to verify the cop's information—to confirm that the shop was owned by a Klansman named John Howard—nor to decide that the best way to fight the store would be to go after the business license. The atmosphere inside Foggie's that afternoon was all the confirmation he needed that things would likely spin out of control. There was too much idle chatter about breaking the shop windows, too much tough talk about confronting the Klan in the streets. The younger generation, especially, seemed poised to take matters into their own hands. If Kennedy could convince city officials to deny the shop a license, the whole issue might be avoided. He had already stopped by City Hall, and in the coming days he would speak out on a local AM radio station. "He was trying to stop it," said Clarence Simpson, then a deacon at Rev. Kennedy's New Beginning Missionary Baptist. "But they went right ahead and did it anyway." In late February, Michael Burden was granted a license for the shop in his name.

In the end, Kennedy wasn't even that surprised, for the African American community was woefully underrepresented in Laurens. A mere three of the city's twenty-eight police officers were black. Out of 187 county government jobs, only sixteen were held by black people. He'd seen the response from leadership back in 1994, when a small multiracial church in the hamlet of Ware Shoals—Full Gospel Tabernacle—experienced harassment and intimidation by the Klan after hiring a black associate pastor: "If Pastor Brown is saying that law enforcement is not dealing with this situation," Laurens County sheriff Jim Moore had complained to the Greenwood *Index-Journal*, "then he's either terribly misinformed or he's trying to mislead the public." Kennedy was used to denial and indifference in the face of prejudice. He wasn't through fighting—not by a long shot.

But despite his best efforts, the shop on the square was going to open right on schedule.

JOHN HOWARD AND Michael Burden had done their best to keep the true nature of the store a secret. As the grand opening approached, however, they began to realize that operating the Redneck Shop in full public view might prove trickier than they had imagined. "We'd already heard the scuttlebutt around town," Burden said. He knew some kind of protest or demonstration was likely, and that the outspoken reverend would surely be the man behind it. So long as those demonstrations didn't interfere with his business, he was inclined to live and let live. As for public opinion, he couldn't have cared less if the residents of Laurens had a problem with the Klan. "I'd put on this shirt," he said, referring to a stretched-out graphic tee emblazoned with a Confederate flag, a pickup truck, and a crass slogan printed along the bottom: IT'S A WHITE THING. YOU WOULDN'T UNDERSTAND. "I'd walk in the middle of Walmart and dare somebody to say something to me. I didn't give a shit."

But for all his posturing, there was one thing about which he had definitely come to care about over the course of the previous few months. That was Judy.

They had technically met several years earlier, long before she'd shown up unannounced at the Echo theater, back when she was living in the Town and Country trailer park with her husband, Carl, and her two children. Burden had been on his way to visit a friend—Judy's next-door neighbor—when he came upon the petite brunette in the middle of an epic rant, cussing up a storm and waving her cigarette in the air, all fire and fury. "She'd had issues with a bus driver or something,"

Burden said later. "And she was madder than hell, raisin hell out in the front yard, and I come over there like, 'Hey, what's goin on?' Ya know?"

Even then he liked her. She had a heart-shaped face, steely blue eyes, and—when she wasn't on a profanity-laced tear—a wide smile. It didn't take him long to invite her to a meeting. She was, after all, a prospective recruit.

It wasn't the first time Judy had been propositioned by a Klansman. In fact, the Klan was relatively pervasive in Laurens, particularly in the trailer parks and textile mills, and among people Judy refers to as "living the hustle-bustle, day-to-day life. Lower-class, like me." Growing up, virtually all of her friends' parents had been members, though at the time Judy had no knowledge of the Klan's violent history, nor even a clear understanding of the group's purpose. "I thought about it like a club that the older adults went to, like the Shriners," she said. By the time she reached adolescence, many of her friends had followed in their parents' footsteps, and they began pressuring Judy to join, too, explaining that it was everyone's responsibility to ensure the safety and security of the white race.

To be sure, casual racism—even overt racism—was very much the norm in Judy's social circle. She was a young woman before it dawned on her that the word "nigger," tossed off with alarming frequency by virtually everyone she knew, was actually a pejorative. "I just thought it was normal to hear that word come out of everybody," she says. "But as I started gettin up older, I realized people were sayin that over a color of the skin, and that's just not right."

Burden was different. He didn't say much about race—not in that first meeting, at least—but talked instead about southern history and pride in one's heritage. She still turned him down.

She was married, for one thing, and even then it was clear that the tattooed stranger was interested in procuring more than her membership. But she couldn't deny that he had made her curious. Burden was long and sinewy, full of bravado but oddly charming, and young—seven years her junior.

She ran into him from time to time after that, but it wasn't until her marriage faltered in late 1995 that she went looking for him at the Echo. "He made the Klan sound more like a family than a hate group," she says. And after her divorce, with two young children to support, a family was what Judy desperately needed. "When me and Carl busted up," she said, "that's when me and Mike started flirtin.'"

Their courtship began almost immediately, but it didn't take long for Judy to confirm that she had been right about the Klan. It was decidedly *not* for her, though the first meeting she attended—at Mike's urging—had been relatively uneventful. The big room on the second floor of the Lanford house was maybe half full, fifteen or twenty people talking quietly and hanging out, just like normal. When Mike called the meeting to order, however, with a sharp rap of what looked like a gavel against the podium, conversation ceased immediately. At his prompting, some of the men came forward and began to assemble items atop a makeshift altar—an American flag, a sword, a Bible.

"Your Excellency," one of them bellowed, "the sacred altar of the Klan is prepared; the fiery cross illuminates the klavern." The "fiery cross," in this case, was a four-foot-tall wooden cross studded with lightbulbs.

It was more pomp and circumstance than Judy was used to—she hadn't quite been prepared to hear strangers refer to her boyfriend as "Your Excellency"—but the whole thing struck her as an elaborate game of dress-up or role-play. The week's "business" turned out to be fairly innocuous: talk consisted mainly of progress reports on renovations at the shop. "I was like, 'Well, there ain't much to this,'" she said.

Her opinion changed three meetings later, when it came time to formally initiate the most recent batch of recruits. "The next thing I know, there's somebody pullin out a cattle prod and just stickin it to them: to their back, their legs." She wanted to protest, but the recruits had been ordered not to speak unless spoken to. And though the men were mostly laughing and joking and carrying on, though *she* was never poked or prodded, Judy was genuinely scared. Most everyone was armed with a handgun, holstered at his side. John Howard was traveling with a pack of five or six men, as a form of protection. It occurred to her that Mike and John had both been breaking her in slowly, revealing the truth about the Klan's nature a little at a time so as not to scare her off.

"I was like, *this* is what everybody's been talkin about? Uh-uh. No way," she said later. After that meeting, when she and Mike were alone, she unloaded. "I said, 'I really have feelings for you, but I cannot have myself or my kids around . . . such crap as this.'"

At thirty-three years old, with no job and two kids to support, she had enough trouble on her hands without having to worry about being poked in the rear end with a cattle prod.

Judy Harbeson (née Gray) was born in the fall of 1962, the seventh child in a large, blended family. She'd gotten pregnant at sixteen and adopted out her son, Ricky, to his paternal grandfather, as she felt she was too young to properly care for him. A year later, she was married to a different man and pregnant with baby number two—but that relationship ended before the end of her first trimester. By the time her second child turned one,

Judy had taken up with Carl, an employee at a paper and specialty fabric manufacturer in the neighboring town of Clinton.

Out of high school now, Judy got a job in the mills, too, just like her grandmother and grandfather, her aunts and uncles, and her mother and sister before her. "When I went in there," Judy said, "I'm left-handed, and they told me: 'You'll never be able to weave.'" By which her bosses meant she might have difficulty tying weaver's knots—tiny knots used to join new thread or to repair broken threads, small enough to pass through a loom undetected. Weavers tie thousands of them each shift, but it's a two-handed job and can sometimes be tricky for lefties. Judy, however, was not someone who easily took no for an answer. "I said, '*Yes, I can.*'" And so she did. She so excelled in her training, her managers often pulled her off the floor and brought her back to class to teach new employees.

For the next thirteen years, Judy worked the third shift—from midnight to eight—monitoring production in a warehouse-like space vibrating with the *clackita-clackita-clackita* of nearly two hundred looms. Her association with the mill, however, hardly ended when she clocked out for the day. For thousands of workers in Laurens County, in fact, life utterly revolved around the mills—socially, spiritually, financially.

"They had what they call the company store," Judy explained. "You could buy food, clothes, furniture. You could go in there and say, 'I want to charge this to a payday.' That's how us mill workers survived. Say it was the middle of the week and you broke. You need, like, bread, milk, cereal? You could go to the company store and tell 'em, 'Put it on my account.' . . . I'd watch my sister go in there and actually buy Christmas for her kids, and put it on a weekly plan."

With Carl, Judy conceived two more children: Carla, who arrived early (weighing just a pound and a half) and died shortly after birth, and Stacy, born in the summer of 1985, just a month shy of Judy's twenty-third birthday. Like many in the community, she relied on the company store to help provide for her family. But by the mid-1990s, the wave of mill closures raging across the Upstate had finally reached Laurens. The shuttering of the Lydia Mill and the Laurens Glass factory—announced within weeks of each other—would go on to put eight hundred people out of work. "One minute you had a job, and the next it was gone," Judy said. "It was that fast."

She bounced from odd job to odd job, starting with a gig working the register at a convenience store. But even when she could find work, it was hardly enough to survive on, especially without the crutch of the company store. And though Carl proved a dutiful co-parent even after the breakup, child support for Stacy amounted to just thirty dollars a week.

Not that Michael Burden could offer her much better. He had no real job to speak of, as he wasn't really paid for his time at Plantation Concrete. What little money he did manage to scrape together was shunted into the fledgling downtown business. But there was something about him. Away from the Klan—in particular, away from the watchful eyes of John Howard—he dropped his tough-guy facade. He was suddenly tender and attentive, prone to making grand romantic gestures: leaving a single rose on her pillow or writing pages-long love notes, even drawing her baths and ironing her clothes for her. He was sweet with her kids. On their first official date, Burden had invited Judy and the children to spend the afternoon with him at Lake Greenwood. She thought she saw something in him that perhaps no one else did. "When we were by ourself and the Klan wasn't involved, he was a totally different person," she said. "I already had it in my mind to get him away from it."

In the meantime, Burden found himself juggling the demands of his new girlfriend and those of his old boss. Every moment he wasn't with Judy, he was down at the shop, preparing for the imminent grand opening. He hauled in glass display cases and filled them with 1920s-era patches and pins and Klan calling cards ("You've been visited by the Ku Klux Klan. This was a social call. Please don't make the next visit a business call"). Howard's old studio portrait—the 1970s-era photo of him dressed in full Klan robes—was given prominent placement on the wall behind the register. Curiosities were stacked willy-nilly atop every available surface: cement statues of Klansmen trucked over from Plantation Concrete, segregation-era signs—NO DOGS, NEGROES, MEXICANS. In one corner of the room, a small television played *The Birth of a Nation* on loop.

Howard, meanwhile, took pains to bestow legitimacy on the whole enterprise. After Burden's promotion to Grand Dragon, he had given himself a new title: Imperial Emperor of Fraternal Rites, a keeper of Klan traditions and ceremonial proceedings. He started to portray himself as something of an amateur historian—a clever way of disavowing the Klan's legacy of violence and bigotry. In opening the Redneck Shop and the soon-to-be-completed museum, he told the press, he was merely preserving records and documents for posterity.

Judy knew better. She'd seen the "exhibits," including one featuring a black mannequin lying in an old casket with a noose around its neck. In the coming weeks, when word of the grotesque display ripped through town, Howard would deny the display's very existence, going so far as to claim it was actually a white mannequin dressed in a black robe. The whole installation, he said, was merely a way of symbolizing "that the Klan was dead."

Judy remembers it differently. "It was a black mannequin," she said, shaking her head. "And it *did* have a rope around its neck. They wanted to cause a scene. They thought it was funny."

Judy had always known the store would cause a stir, but even she underestimated the effect her boyfriend's business would have on Laurens. Because within days of the Redneck Shop's grand opening, hell broke loose.

"Are their sole motives to display history?"

Ed McDaniel, a prominent local businessman and one of only two African Americans on the Laurens County Council, had been suspicious of the Redneck Shop from the start. As soon as the doors opened on Friday, March 1—as soon as he caught a glimpse of the Klansman's robe positioned prominently in the shop window—he, too, started to speak out. It wasn't the first time he'd squared off with members of the Klan. Decades earlier, he'd spent more than one evening watching over his family's home, in the event that local boys from the hooded order felt like doing a little night-riding. He was, somewhat ironically, a collector of Klan memorabilia, a reminder of that harrowing time in his own history. So when it came to John Howard and his brand-new business, McDaniel had no trouble admitting that he took personal offense.

He also knew that the situation, already explosive, would only get worse. McDaniel had been a senior at historically black South Carolina State University in the winter of 1968, when three African American teenagers—two SCSU students and a local high-schooler—were shot to death by members of the Highway Patrol during an on-campus demonstration against a local segregated bowling alley. The tragic scandal would come to be known as the Orangeburg Massacre. He knew better than most just how quickly activism could become deadly.

In the first five days alone, police had been summoned to the Redneck Shop twice to break up minor disturbances. The storefront had been pelted with rocks, eggs, and bricks. The mannequin positioned in the window, meanwhile, had caused such outrage that Howard had no choice but to move it to the back of the shop. A special agent from the State Law Enforcement Division had been dispatched to "take the pulse" of the community. The story about the Ku Klux Klan museum in the little southern town had already gone national—the square was awash with reporters and news cameras. Traffic was clogged. And Howard, the man who started it all, had been all too eager to put the blame on anyone but himself. "I didn't mean for this to take place," he told the *Laurens County Advertiser.* "I wanted to sell a few things—not to offend anyone and not to glorify the Klan. I did not realize the black race was so prejudiced about this. I'm very sorry we've caused any trouble. All I ask is for the respect I give them"—by which Howard meant the respect he'd given *African Americans.*

It was a ridiculous assertion, and McDaniel wasn't having it. "Ignoring the Redneck Shop and hoping it goes away is a mistake," he said. It was Tuesday, March 12, the first regularly scheduled County Council meeting since the grand opening. McDaniel had expected a larger-than-average turnout, and he wasn't disappointed. Residents had packed themselves into the council chambers, an auditorium on the second floor of the county courthouse.

McDaniel wasn't a particularly large man. With his high forehead and bushy mustache, he bore an uncanny resemblance to a 1970s-era Sherman Hemsley, but he nonetheless cut a stately figure in Laurens. He was known throughout town as a man of great integrity, possessed of both wit and wisdom. Prejudice, however, was never very far from his mind. McDaniel had yet to see folks in Laurens denounce racism, nor reckon with their past. "I haven't had the general citizenry of Laurens County stand up in my lifetime and say this is morally wrong," he said.

McDaniel spoke at length about the necessity of addressing issues of race openly, stressing that it was a moral responsibility on the part of his fellow council members. It was also, he said, an economic matter. In the wake of the Lydia Mill and Laurens Glass closures, the county was in desperate need of investment dollars. Geographically, Laurens was positioned to attract exactly that. Drawn by favorable tax rates, easy access to the deepwater port of Charleston, a rock-bottom cost of living, and a century of anti-union policies, foreign companies including BMW and Michelin had already started to dump millions of dollars into the northwest corner of the state. *Site Selection* magazine, a trade publication for corporate executives and real estate professionals, would soon rank five Upstate towns—all in the Greenville-Spartanburg metro area—among the top twenty cities nationwide for foreign direct investment. The existence of the Redneck Shop, however, could jeopardize any hope Laurens had of righting itself. McDaniel reminded his fellow council members that representatives of one foreign company had recently asked how their nationality and culture would be viewed by local residents, should they relocate to the area. McDaniel's question was a simple one: What in the world do we tell them?

Beyond speaking out, though, McDaniel didn't have much in the way of real options. Michael Burden had filed for and been granted a business license. Even if city administrators hadn't fully grasped the nature of the shop, there were no ordinances on the books preventing such a business from operating within city or county limits. Forcibly shutting down the Redneck Shop, much as that was exactly what McDaniel would have liked to do, would be a legal nightmare in the making. (As a fellow councilman warned: "We are treading on dangerous ground if we're talking about violating [Howard's] First, Fifth, and possibly Ninth Amendment rights.") So instead, McDaniel urged his fellow council members to do the only thing they really *could* do: draft a resolution condemning the shop, the Ku Klux Klan, and everything the Klan stood for. It would be little more than a symbolic gesture, but one McDaniel felt they needed to make. Remaining silent, he said, would only "lend credence to the KKK."

As he reached the end of his prepared remarks, McDaniel gestured to a small ribbon pinned to his lapel. In the twelve days since the shop opened, he had talked with those closest to him about how best to turn a bad situation on its head. "We were saying we have a lemon here," he later told the *Laurens County Advertiser*. "How do we turn it into lemonade?" The awareness ribbon—two strands, one black and one white, intertwined to represent racial unity—had been the brainchild of his wife, Sheila, and his mother, Ethel. McDaniel expressed that he hoped folks in town would join him in wearing one.

Almost immediately, the "unity ribbon" campaign seemed like a hit. Thirty-six hours after the County Council meeting, McDaniel estimated that as many as three thousand had been made up and handed out. Two local AM-radio DJs drummed up publicity for the cause on their morning talk show, and a slew of local businesses donated materials. By Wednesday afternoon, ribbons adorned the lapels of school district personnel and government workers, and streamed from the antennae of cars passing through the square. A large black-and-white bow had even been affixed to the front door of City Hall.

But for all the feel-good talk about unity and tolerance and coming together, there was still no consensus about how best to deal with the troublesome shop on the square. Laurens City police chief Robin Morse was indifferent. "If everything runs smoothly," he told reporters, "I've got no beef with Howard." A growing number of residents, meanwhile, seemed convinced that ignoring the shop was the most appropriate response, that giving Howard the publicity they imagined he craved would only prolong the controversy. "I think we need to be together and united about this thing," a Laurens woman told Channel 7 News, "so that we can get back to our normal lives."

And that's exactly why McDaniel had proposed his resolution—getting back to "normal" would mean restoring the very environment that fostered the store in the first place.

In the March 15 edition of the *Laurens County Advertiser*, printed right alongside an editorial condemning the shop, was the "Your Two Cents" column. It was a regular feature in which readers could call in to the paper and leave an anonymous phone message, weighing in on any number of issues. And judging from that week's published responses, not everyone in town had a problem with the shop.

This is concerning the Redneck store. I don't see anything wrong with it. They have stores that sell Malcolm X shirts and black power shirts and Farrakhan shirts and so on, and there's no big to-do about that. So I don't know why they're all upset about the Redneck store. The man's trying to make a little money.

This is about The Redneck Shop on the Square. While I might not agree with the theme of the store, I disagree with the way blacks in the community are reacting to it. He is an American just like they are, and he has every right to run a business as long as he is within the laws of the land. And the man has done nothing wrong and I believe that blacks in the community—if they will look—they will understand that he is just a businessman doing business. And that's my opinion. That's my two cents worth.

I'm calling concerning this Ku Klux Klan over here on the Square. I'm so glad that thing come to Laurens that I don't know what to do, and I think that the white people was sitting back letting these blacks tell the whites what to do and what they can't do, when they have black television. They have black colleges and they have anything they want but they don't want the white people to have anything. And I'm behind the Ku Klux Klan, the redneck store here in Laurens—I'm behind it, 100 percent.

At the council meeting, McDaniel had warned that the media was already portraying Laurens as a backward town, the "last bastion of the Southern tolerance for white supremacy." But no amount of impassioned speeches or unity ribbons could hide the fact that Laurens had a serious race problem.

On assignment for a Sacramento-based alternative weekly, journalist Mike Pulley traveled to Laurens for an up-close-and-personal look at the old Echo theater. After chatting with John Howard—hearing more about his attempts to "educate" folks about the history of the Klan—the reporter stopped in to a local gas station. Moments later, a young black man popped his head in the door and asked the cashier for a book of matches. The cashier, whom Pulley described as a "codger," responded tersely, before turning back to his white patron, "They gettin independent as a devil, ain't they?"

Then he reached into the till and pulled out a small handgun. "I tell you what, if he messes with me too much, I'll give him some of *that.*"

WHILE MCDANIEL WAS busy urging the County Council to condemn racism, Rev. Kennedy watched, somewhat awestruck, as press coverage of the Redneck Shop went national. In between ringing up patrons at the register and monitoring the sidewalk for signs of trouble, Mike Burden was busy fielding media inquiries from NBC News, the *Today* show, a slew of regional and national newspapers, and about a dozen different radio stations. Producers from *Jerry Springer* had called seven separate times. John Howard, meanwhile, had started telling reporters that he knew just "how a black person felt in the '40s and '50s" because he, too, was being discriminated against (a claim he made while wearing—without a trace of irony—a T-shirt printed with the words AIN'T RACIST, JUST NEVER MET A NIGGER I LIKED). He also told the local paper that he'd been threatened by "a local black minister" whose congregation, according to Howard, had used foul language and prejudiced talk against the white race.

Howard didn't bother using Kennedy's name, because he didn't have to. "You can't live in Laurens and not know Reverend Kennedy," Burden explained. "He's like your Al Sharpton. I don't say that in a bad way—I mean, that's how popular he is. I mean, *he slapped the mayor in the middle of town.*"

As soon as he'd gotten word about the license, Kennedy

started planning how best to respond to the birth of the Redneck Shop. There was no question that he would organize protests and rallies and marches—and not just as a matter of principle. "The Klan has always been a deceptive organization," he said. If this was how Klansmen were behaving in public, he could only imagine what might be going on behind closed doors.

At the same time, he wasn't quite sure what to expect from leaders within the black community. Not everyone was a fan of Kennedy's aggressive, in-your-face style. Back in 1990, when he'd led the protests against discrimination in the schools and police brutality and Bobo Cook's death, an African American City Council member, Marian Miller, had publicly admonished him. "Project Awakening wants to get people stirred up," she told the *Greenville News,* stressing that patience and dialogue were the more appropriate ways to solve such problems.

Rev. Kennedy was not about to be patient. But he'd also spoken with many members of his congregation, and while virtually everyone was angry and disgusted and deeply upset, quite a few were just plain scared. His first order of business, then, was hosting a community meeting at the church in order to address those fears, as well as to organize the official response to the shop. Kennedy was surprised—but pleased—to see Councilwoman Miller among the crowd.

Like McDaniel, Miller had been a student at South Carolina State during the Orangeburg Massacre. She still had scars on her knees from crawling her way to safety that night. So she urged those planning to rally against the Redneck Shop to be both careful and cautious. "It is time for us to open our eyes," she said. "But we don't know who will be there, and it might be someone who wants us to act up. They might be looking for a confrontation. We aren't going to give them that."

Rev. Kennedy echoed that sentiment at his first official protest rally the following Saturday. "If somebody rides by and
starts calling names," he shouted into the mic, "let the cops
handle it. If any of you have violence in you, we're asking you to
leave. We're not about that."

Nearly four hundred demonstrators, young and old, black
and white, had gathered in defiance of racism. They came wearing their unity ribbons and bearing signs that read KKK IS NOT
WELCOME IN THIS COUNTY and NO TOLERANCE FOR HATE. Five
dozen cops, meanwhile, from at least four separate state and
local agencies, were stationed around the square. Kennedy led
the crowd in prayer and call-and-response chants and his famous "pump it up" song ("Everybody got to pump / Pump it /
Pump it up!"). He welcomed speaker after speaker to the makeshift stage. He condemned those who had failed to act in light
of worsening race relations. "To my critics," he said, "you had a
chance to do something and you didn't."

It wasn't until later that the reverend heard about the near-
arrest. While Kennedy was praising his "white brothers and
sisters" for joining the fight, authorities were questioning a suspicious character who turned out to be transporting military-
grade walkie-talkies, baseball bats, a handgun, and a Klan robe
in his truck. They let him go, however, because "nothing he had
was illegal."

Rev. Jesse Jackson, a Greenville native, had been in town
visiting family when he heard about the controversy. On Sunday, he met with ministers across the Upstate region to discuss strategy. By Monday he was in Laurens, holding a press
conference outside New Beginning Missionary Baptist, urging
residents not to back down. "It is not just the symbol, but the
act of recruitment of people to titillate their fears, so this group

brought in caskets with black mannequins in the caskets, and ropes around the necks of the mannequins, to demonstrate a threat and an act of intimidation, and the police and judges should not rest easy when that happens. If there is silence," Jackson warned, "they will manifest themselves in the police department, they will manifest themselves in the judiciary, they will manifest themselves in the church." He announced that he had contacted Attorney General Janet Reno and requested that she launch a federal investigation into the shop.

The demonstrations that week generated far more attention than any of Kennedy's previous protests. But in the immediate aftermath of the first rally, the demands of his day job took precedence over the new cause. The Soup Kitchen, which operated out of an industrial kitchen in the rear of his church, served an average of 225 meals every day, prepared and delivered entirely by volunteers. If the church van broke down—and it often did—someone had to make sure that Alberta, his aunt and head cook, had a ride in the morning.

During the day, Kennedy was notoriously difficult to schedule a meeting with. Any time someone within a three-county radius called for help—and someone *always* called—he would leap into his car and speed off, no matter who might've been waiting to see him. It was not unusual to find a line of people queued up outside Kennedy's office door, with no idea when he might be back. And these days the line seemed longer than usual. Younger parishioners started dropping by, angry and indignant about the shop on the square—the fact that it was still open for business, despite the protests. One evening, however, he took an impromptu meeting that left him more distressed than the others. A local school bus driver had shown up at the church and plopped himself down in the chair across from Kennedy. "He was wild-eyed," the reverend remembers, "and I said, 'Oh, Lord, what's wrong?' He told me that he was tired, and he was crying."

"Rev," the driver asked, "why they treat us like this all the time?"

"They have something in them, telling them that they are superior. That they are better than us."

"Will it ever change?"

"No," Kennedy said. "Never. Not till Jesus come back."

A different sort of minister might've offered more comfort, but placating his parishioners, especially when it came to matters of race, was not Kennedy's style. The two men sat for a long while, until the driver said quietly, "I want to burn it down."

It was not the first time that Rev. Kennedy heard someone in the community threaten violence. "I told him, 'Fight *with* me. Join with me. Don't burn it down. Give me your word.'" But the meeting left him feeling uneasy. He started to believe that some kind of major altercation was inevitable, that it was only a matter of time before he got word that someone was in serious trouble down at the shop.

The only surprising part was how quickly the call came.

It was Sunday, March 24, a little over a week after the first rally. Gregory Fielder, the owner of a nearby car wash, watched in stunned silence as a white 1975 Ford van backed into the Redneck Shop's storefront at high speed, crushing display cases and clothing racks, sending shards of glass glittering across the pavement. The van rolled forward and then slammed into reverse, ramming through the shop windows again and again and again. Fielder was already on the phone with police when a middle-aged white man emerged from the van, climbed onto its roof, and started beating the Echo's old metal marquee with a hickory stick.

The vigilante turned out not to be a member of Kennedy's congregation. He wasn't even a resident of Laurens, in fact, but rather a forty-three-year-old carpet installer from Columbia named David Prichard Hunter. He was regarded by friends and family alike as something of a hippie pacifist—the incident with the van was deemed profoundly out of character. Yet even after police took him into custody, Hunter expressed no remorse for what he'd done.

"I think it's better to do this than, six months from now, to have to look at the face of an anguished black woman on television whose son has been hung from a tree and tortured," he said. "I want to tell the rest of America that apathy ain't going to get us anywhere. If no one takes a stand, a stand won't be taken."

Hunter had actually made the hour-and-a-half drive to Laurens once before—five days before the incident—staying just long enough to peek in the windows of the empty shop before turning around and heading back home. It wasn't until Sunday morning, after reading yet another article about the controversy, that he snapped.

Word spread quickly. McDaniel was on the square within minutes, passing out more of his unity ribbons. The street was roped off by police, and a crowd gathered to gawk at the scene. But when it became clear that no one was injured—Hunter had apparently confirmed that the shop was empty before driving through it—the general vibe downtown shifted from fear and concern to something more like schadenfreude. "While we cannot condone willful destruction of anyone's property," McDaniel told reporters, "in my heart, I cannot tell you I'm sorry it happened."

Rev. Kennedy likewise stressed to reporters the importance

of nonviolent resistance ("We disagree with the method") but nonetheless met with Hunter and helped him raise the funds to make bail. As for Hunter's family, they weren't exactly upset. "This was madcap," his brother Kevin admitted to the *Greenville News*, "but I'm kind of proud of him."

Michael Burden, on the other hand, was livid. He'd arrived on the scene later that morning to find shattered antiques and display cases, merchandise strewn across the sidewalk, books and charters and other irreplaceable Klan relics completely destroyed. "I wanted to kill the SOB," he said. Before a crowd of roughly two hundred onlookers—many of them straight from church, dressed in their Sunday best—Burden set about boarding up the windows and doors and piling up items into the back of the shop to be sorted through later. Mad as he was, he and Howard took comfort in the fact that they weren't alone. "We had people all the way from Spartanburg come down and they were helping us put the place back together," he said. "We had one lady from Laurens, she actually took materials—shirts and stuff that's been thrown out into the street—she took 'em to her house and washed 'em and brought 'em back, and we hung 'em up again." Most of the helpers were either fellow Klansmen or Klan sympathizers—all were white—but there were enough people on hand to make quick work of getting the Redneck Shop back in business; the store reopened inside of eight hours, with the windows and doors boarded up.

Speaking to reporters, John Howard claimed that he'd already forgiven Hunter "from the bottom of my heart." But behind closed doors, he was gearing up for battle. Six additional security cameras were set up around the perimeter of the building. (The preexisting two had captured the entire episode with the van, and the footage had been shared with Laurens police.) Howard and Burden started spending nights at the shop, staying up until one or two o'clock in the morning, watching TV on a small set in the back hall near the restrooms and the water fountain, just waiting for someone else to come along and wreak more havoc. The longer they sat there, the more Burden was made to believe that the van was just the beginning of the violence, and that whatever else might be coming their way, Rev. Kennedy would be the man behind it. "The best weapon John had was me," Burden said. "And the best way to get me activated was to make me believe my life and my livelihood was in jeopardy. He knew what buttons to push."

Judy heard Howard goading Mike into action, too. "He always used to tell him—and I heard him, quote unquote: 'Mike, you got to do something. That nigger is like a thorn in my side. You hear me, boy?'"

five

NON SILBA SED ANTHAR

For a brief moment that spring, immediately following David
Prichard Hunter's decision to plow his van into the front of the
Redneck Shop, there was in Laurens a certain sense of levity—
a feeling, almost, of victory within reach. Even with all the
drama and turmoil, residents seemed to be talking more, making active efforts to "fix" the way in which their town was being
portrayed around the world.

Ed McDaniel, however, wondered aloud if Hunter's actions—
though lauded by many as nothing short of heroic—might have
been too good to be true. In fact, he wondered, what if John
Howard was *in* on it? "Could this be something contrived to get
enough money to open his museum?" he mused to a reporter
from the Associated Press.

Technically, the museum was already open—just small, rel-
egated to the corridor in the back of the shop, not yet fully realized. Howard's plan had always been to finish renovating the
cavernous screening room and relocate the exhibits there. In
fact, he insisted that the store was merely a means of financing

the larger mission. "I'm just trying to tell the truth of what took place," he'd said back in early March. "The good, the bad, and the ugly of it. I'm not trying to lift [the Klan] up."

Still, McDaniel's theory wasn't exactly far-fetched. As part of Hunter's preliminary hearing, Howard claimed nearly $15,000 worth of damage to the shop—more than $9,000 in losses to personal property, another $5,000 in damage to the building itself. The problem with that figure, as Hunter's defense attorney Duffie Stone pointed out, was that a Laurens city tax assessor's notice had pegged the value of the building *and* the land at just $5,200. "I don't believe there is any allegation that the building was burned to the ground and the land scarred," Stone said in court. "It appears to me that what Howard is doing is over-inflating the damage to the building." Outside the courtroom, Stone's dismissal of the charges bordered on outright sarcasm: "I can't imagine that particular type of merchandise being worth fifty cents, much less ten thousand dollars."

The Klan has always traded on fear and intimidation—or, at least, spectacle—as a means of gaining power. Howard, in particular, was a known provocateur. But even he hadn't expected opposition to the shop—and to him personally—to escalate so rapidly. In a matter of days, Janet Reno's team at the Department of Justice agreed to launch an investigation into possible civil rights violations by the Redneck Shop. According to the local papers, a Laurens bank had asked John Howard to close his account. Whatever the true monetary value of the damages, the shop was certainly a wreck. And now he had a County Council member accusing him, publicly, of insurance fraud.

"John was getting royally pissed off about it," says Burden. For all his years in the Klan, Howard had never been up against this kind of public pressure. He had always served some larger, more notorious Klan figure, and he'd stayed out of serious trouble, in part, by goading his subordinates into action. So it wasn't long before he started suggesting to Burden that something ought to be done about McDaniel.

"Well, he's a councilman," Burden replied, figuring there must be some kind of law against badmouthing one's own constituents. "Why don't you just sue the hell out of him?"

"How?" Howard asked.

"Easy. Get a damn lawyer."

McDANIEL HAD NO way of knowing what sort of trouble might be coming his way. On the contrary, by early April it seemed as though he had plenty to celebrate. Two weeks after hearing his formal proposal, the Laurens County Council voted—unanimously—to pass his anti-Klan resolution, condemning the Ku Klux Klan specifically and organized hate groups in general. The official text made no mention of John Howard or the Redneck Shop, but McDaniel hoped its passage would be viewed by those both inside and outside of town as a significant step. "By your vote tonight," he told his fellow council members, "you have sent a message about Laurens County. You may not know it, but tonight you have fired a shot that in the morning could be heard round the world. You have done something you can look back on and tell your children you were proud to do. You have taken a stand—not against a business, but a belief."

Whatever wave of momentum the resolution might generate—however small—McDaniel intended to ride it. He immediately formed what he dubbed the Unity Ribbon Network and announced what was to be the first of many Unity Forums, invitation-only events meant to facilitate frank discussion about race relations. About twenty-five people, half of those invited, showed up for the first meeting, held in an auxiliary office complex about a mile northeast of the courthouse square. Each member of the group—which included the mayor, the sheriff, school district personnel, various religious leaders, and several members of the media—took his or her seat within a circle of chairs, and after a bit of prompting from McDaniel's wife, the conversation turned deeply personal. Shannon Long, director of missions for the Laurens Baptist Association, remembered playing baseball as a child with kids from the neighborhood—black and white—until someone informed his mother, and that was the end of that. Gregory Fielder, the local business owner who'd phoned the police after Hunter plowed his van into the shop, shared his belief that America had always been a racist nation: "Ninety-nine percent of the history books are incorrect, and this is what we are teaching our children," he said. McDaniel participated, too, reminding the attendees that "if you're forty years old and honest, you'll admit that there was at one time an unspoken rule that blacks didn't look at a white man." His focus, however, seemed to be more about finding common ground with the majority-white crowd than highlighting issues of systemic inequality. "Everybody's been exposed to prejudice," he said, rather charitably.

For one member of the group—Reverend Kennedy—McDaniel's approach left much to be desired. David Prichard Hunter, after all, had resorted to violence because he believed the town wasn't doing enough to root out racism; he claimed he was taking a stand against apathy. Having a closed-door, invitation-only chat, then, hardly seemed like the best way to demonstrate that Laurens was addressing its issues head-on. It also flew in the face of Rev. Kennedy's personal message, which was that no one in Laurens could escape responsibility for the environment that had fostered the Redneck Shop. In the previous weeks, he had railed against religious leaders for being too passive, frequently telling the press that it would "take a lot more than prayer" to solve the town's race problem. He distrusted most civil servants, who he claimed were "more concerned about economics than the devastating psychological impact the KKK has on an entire race of African Americans." He had called on law enforcement to increase surveillance of the Redneck Shop—to "step up its pace"—a subtle jab at officers who had allowed the Klan to flourish under their noses.

After sitting in the meeting and listening to the first couple of speakers, he stormed out—only to return a few hours later and then storm out again. His second appearance, during which he claimed the group was not having a "true dialogue," effectively and abruptly ended the event (a gossipy tidbit that didn't escape mention by the local press). "There are a number of people who are in a rage because this could have been handled differently," he said to reporters afterward.

Though both men were united in their opposition to Howard's shop, the rift between McDaniel and Kennedy introduced into the larger controversy a question of ownership: Who owned the protests and marches, and the movement they produced? In the days immediately following Rev. Jesse Jackson's appearance in Laurens, when press coverage focused more on Jackson's celebrity status than the dark history of the Klan or the efforts of the community, Kennedy had been quick to reclaim the issue as a local one. "We don't want to lose sight of whose fight this is," he told the *Clinton Chronicle*. "We will ask [Jackson] to return when we've gotten some work done."

When it came to local-level leadership, however, it wasn't

really clear who was in charge—McDaniel or Kennedy. Their styles could not have been more different. McDaniel was conservative and reserved, more interested in calming things down than riling people up. "He always had a passion for equality among the races," said Jim Coleman, who served alongside McDaniel on the council for twenty years. "He would always bring that up, but he would do it in a very professional manner." Kennedy, on the other hand, was the protest minister. He was loud, angry, unapologetic. He wanted people to look hard issues in the face. But even in the first weeks of the controversy, it must have felt as though whatever control he had of the situation was already being wrested away from him.

McDaniel's Unity Ribbon campaign, for example, had received glowing press coverage. But while Kennedy's initial rally had been largely praised, others were suggesting that the protests be moved away from the square, because Kennedy was generating undue attention for the Redneck Shop. "Some people in Laurens, they called it a disgrace," he later recalled. "They blamed *me* for bringing top publicity to the place. You know, 'The biggest problem in Laurens County is David Kennedy.'"

He knew it wasn't uncommon for protesters to take more heat than the thing they were protesting. But Kennedy also believed that you generally had to make people uncomfortable to generate meaningful change. His version of the fight, then, would be the very opposite of a private meeting. It would have to be as public as possible.

With a small contingent of local ministers, Rev. Kennedy appeared before South Carolina's Legislative Black Caucus and urged its members to condemn the Redneck Shop specifically— as opposed to racism in general—and stressed the importance of "militant nonviolence" as a strategy. It was a page out of

Martin Luther King Jr.'s playbook. Time had already softened the sharpest edges of King's most radical rhetoric, but the image of him as a crowd-pleasing pacifist—a "civil rights teddy bear," as Rev. Jackson once observed—obscures the fact that he was polarizing and divisive in his time, and his methods deeply controversial. Ten days before his death, while speaking at the annual convention of the Rabbinical Assembly in New York, he professed his belief in the power of disruption: "I can't see the answer in riots. On the other hand, I can't see the answer in tender supplications for justice. I see the answer in an alternative to both of these, and that is militant nonviolence that is massive enough, that is attention-getting enough, to dramatize the problems, that will be as attention-getting as a riot, that will not destroy life or property in the process." In his own way, Kennedy's style—the antagonism, the willingness to offend—had also, always, been about disruption as a means of subverting the status quo.

As it turned out, the members of the Black Caucus were likewise interested in disruption, in part because fighting the Redneck Shop could be turned into something of a referendum on the governor of South Carolina, David Beasley.

Only sixteen months into office, Beasley's relationship with the caucus had already turned rocky. Not long after his inauguration, assembly members had voiced concerns that he was failing to appoint enough African Americans to key posts and positions. Then, in the summer of 1995, black lawmakers alleged that Beasley had threatened to veto their entire legislative agenda—some $7.2 million earmarked for welfare reform, programs at South Carolina State University, and African American studies at the University of South Carolina—if they didn't vote with Republicans on issues coming before the General Assembly (a charge Beasley did not deny). By fall, the only African American woman on the governor's staff, a legislative liaison named Wilma Neal, had resigned, citing ostracism and exclusion from even the most routine of meetings. Beasley needed to rehabilitate his image—and fast. In December, he announced the formation of a Race Relations Commission to "tear down [the] wall" of racial division, only to anger everyone all over again by declaring two weeks later, at a summit organized by the Palmetto Project, that race relations in South Carolina were "good."

"Race relations . . . today are more tense, more filled with fear, frustration, and anger than they have been at any time in a generation," Representative Ralph Canty, a Democrat from Sumter, said at a press conference. As he and other members of the caucus well knew, Beasley's image problems and the arrival of the Redneck Shop were far from the only signs of trouble. Something was brewing. In the month of April alone, a white man had been arrested for spray-painting KKK on an African American couple's property outside Charleston; the FBI had launched an investigation into a cross-burning in Canterbury, a mostly black neighborhood in southern Greenville County; and national condemnation poured on the state following the release of dashcam video depicting a white state trooper assaulting a black motorist. There were concerns, too, about a racially motivated wave of church burnings. In the previous eighteen months, fires had been reported at more than sixty predominantly black churches across the South, triggering widespread press coverage and a massive federal investigation.

After Rev. Kennedy's appearance before the Caucus, state senator Maggie Glover called on the governor and both houses of the General Assembly to "loudly and unequivocally" condemn the Redneck Shop. Representative Joe Neal went after Governor Beasley more personally, calling him out for his silence: "Today there is no message from our governor that he understands how injurious the presence of the Redneck Shop is to racial harmony, and thereby to both the human and economic development of our people." Rev. Kennedy, meanwhile, vowed to keep up the momentum at home. He announced plans for a second rally in the courthouse square, and invited the former pastor of Mount Zion Baptist, allegedly burned by the Klan in 1971, to speak. A new sense of urgency had been injected into his speeches and sermons. At a Wednesday-night community meeting, for example, he explained that Howard was using the shop "to recruit members to the KKK and his goal is to create a race war."

It was around this time that Kennedy started bringing reporters down to the old trestle over on River Street. For weeks, he had been sharing the story of his great-uncle's death with his parishioners and members of the community. Back in March, he had tacked a poster-size photo of the Puckett lynching to the front of his pulpit—the same photo that had circulated through town in the 1950s as a deterrent to integration. He had carried it with him at the first major rally against the Redneck Shop in an attempt to shock people out of complacency. "In order to understand why black churches are burning," he explained to a reporter from the Associated Press, "you have to understand how racism happens. America would love to put all the blame on the Ku Klux Klan. But what creates this atmosphere that allows the Klan to become bold?"

For Kennedy, this fight was about more than a store, and the Redneck Shop was more than merely crass or distasteful. The Klan was recruiting. Without some kind of check against it, without a prolonged and continued fight, the shop's presence, and its message, would be normalized. "As long as the Redneck Shop is there," he told reporters, "violence is inevitable."

SUZANNE COE WAS a thirty-one-year-old Greenville-based attorney who had risen to national prominence in 1995 after winning Shannon Faulkner admission to the prestigious—and previously all-male—Citadel military college in Charleston. Her law practice had an emphasis on individual rights cases with a mostly progressive bent. Locally, however, she was best known for a willingness to represent even the least savory of characters. Her client roster included a Lexington County hitman and a former state senator charged with tax evasion. A prominent anti-abortion activist had labeled her "a crusader for the weird and perverse." Coe's ex-husband, fellow attorney Rob Hoskins, once joked: "I honestly believe that she would defend the head of the Ku Klux Klan."

When the head of the Klan came calling, however, she had no interest in taking his case.

Coe, a petite woman with bushy brown hair and what the *Greenville News* once described as "can't-sit-still" energy, had come to John Howard's attention for her defense of a gentlemen's club, Diamonds, which opened outside Greenville in the fall of 1994, to the great consternation of local residents. In response, the Greenville County Council adopted a zoning ordinance regulating the locations of adult entertainment businesses, and then went on to pass an outright ban on public nudity. The fight generated enough press that the Laurens County Council, one month before the Redneck Shop opened its doors, briefly debated adopting a similar ordinance.

Coe, however, had sided with Diamonds—as well as a local

exotic dancer, Melissa Wolf—arguing that the ban on nudity was a violation of free speech. "I see it as, once again, the Baptists come out against dancing," Coe said at the time. "[The club] is going to be there. They might as well get over it and grow up." The case wound up going all the way to the State Supreme Court, where Coe won.

"She's not afraid of controversy," a former colleague once explained to reporters. Though the cases she took often exposed her to negative press and a fair amount of harassment, she had never been one to back down. Still, it took a bit of prodding before she agreed to meet with John Howard. "I was discussing it with my partner," she later told the *New York Times*, "and he said: 'Oh, I see. You only stand up for civil rights you believe in.'"

While Coe tried to wrap her head around the implications of representing a Klansman, John Howard got busy attempting to soften his public image. The boarded-up windows at the shop were replaced with glass, and the words JESUS LOVES EVERYBODY were painted beneath the name of the business. He pledged that the museum would be moved "out of sight"—that is, to the old screening room at the rear of the theater, which had always been his plan—and that the store would soon sell only Confederate-themed trinkets. He also commissioned a large Confederate flag, some five or six feet across, printed with the words HERITTAGE [*sic*] NOT HATE.

The slogan—a way of claiming southern pride without owning the legacy of slavery—had only recently been popularized, thanks to a man named Charles Lunsford, a leader of the largest Confederate heritage group in the States, the Sons of Confederate Veterans (SCV). The group's original mission was to preserve history—specifically, a Lost Cause interpretation of the

Civil War. Its aim, according to its 1896 constitution, was "not to create or foster, in any manner, any feeling against the North, but to hand down to posterity the story of the glory of the men who wore the gray." By the 1990s, however, there was division in the ranks. At issue: a shift from traditional pursuits, such as Civil War reenactments and the maintenance of Confederate gravesites, to a more militant focus on "heritage defense"—in particular, the right to display Confederate flags and symbols in public spaces. Traditionalists in the SCV felt as though the organization was being radicalized and politicized; more activist members, meanwhile, wanted to aggressively prosecute alleged "heritage violations" in court.

The flash point came in 1992, when Georgia's governor, Zell Miller, proposed removing the "southern cross" from the official state flag. Lunsford, in his capacity as "chief of heritage defense" for the SCV, was invited to debate Miller on a radio broadcast of *Larry King Live*, where he expressed concerns that flag removal was the beginning of a slippery slope.

LUNSFORD: In 1986, the NAACP began passing resolutions in their national convention to bring about the eradication of everything Confederate.... We began to see our street names change.... We saw the clamoring to remove Confederate monuments.... What I'm getting at here is this is seen by the vast majority of southern people as nothing more than widespread oppression against our culture.... The vast majority of Georgians do not ... see [the Confederate flag] as a racist symbol.

GOV. MILLER: Well, first of all, let's get the difference between the official symbol of a state—which the flag is—and memorials. Georgia has got many, many memorials to the Confederacy.

We've got over 1,100 historical markers all along our highways. We've got 400 monuments on our county and city squares. We've got three battlefields that are run by the federal parks system, and one battlefield by the state. I am not talking about doing anything with these memorials, because that is history. They are memorials. The flag is the official symbol of what a state is, and a flag should not be offensive to forty percent of its people.

LUNSFORD: Well, Mr. Miller, bear in mind that *you* may not be talking about those monuments, but *somebody* is. . . . You may only be talking about the flag, but each of these monuments you go to throughout the country has their own little set of arguments, and when you look at them in their totality, we are under oppression, and people are beginning to resent that.

Lunsford went on to lament the way in which hate groups, including the Klan, had "co-opted" the flag for nefarious use: "The racists have always carried . . . the Confederate flag, because they are trying to win influence with the southern people, because the southern people *love* that flag," he said. The slogan "Heritage Not Hate" (which Lunsford coined around the same time as the interview) became a way of reclaiming something lost, of restoring some "stolen" honor. But the slogan masks some uncomfortable truths.

For one thing, the SCV has long done business with white supremacists. Its leader during the civil rights era, William McCain, was an avowed segregationist. While president of Mississippi Southern College (now the University of Southern Mississippi), he worked to block the admission of Clyde Kennard, a black Korean War veteran, in 1956, 1957, and 1959—two, three, and five years, respectively, after passage of

Brown v. Board of Education. A year later he made a speech in Chicago, sponsored by the Mississippi State Sovereignty Commission, in which he claimed that southerners "insisted" on living in a segregated society and did not support the rights of black men and women to vote. "The Negroes prefer that control of the government remain in the white man's hands," he said.

As for Charles Lunsford, he was ousted from the SCV in 1994 after giving a speech to the Council of Conservative Citizens, a white supremacist outfit classified by the Southern Poverty Law Center as a hate group. He later joined the Atlanta-based Heritage Preservation Association, which has its own troubled history with issues of race. (In 2003, the president of the HPA's Atlanta branch, Linda Sewell, personally accepted a "certificate of appreciation" from the Klan.)

Criticizing "hate groups" for co-opting your message while at the same time eliciting their support is plainly hypocritical. But in a world where up is down and down is up, it becomes that much easier to peddle outright falsehoods and half truths. After all, most of what Mike Burden learned about southern history—and the history of the Klan—is not so different from the version peddled by the Sons of Confederate Veterans. Only by normalizing Confederate iconography does it become possible to patronize a shop operated by an avowed Klansman in the name of "heritage."

And yet one wonders why John Howard even bothered to soften his image. Because no matter what he said to the press about "preserving history," the outgoing message on his own store's answering machine told a far different story. It was a four-minute-long racist rant—a recording made by none other than Michael Burden—billed as a Klan "hotline." (The phone number was printed on the shop's business cards.) The heart of the message was a recruitment plea: callers were asked if they were ready to turn over the country to "militant blacks" and "nigger hordes" who "want to breed with your beautiful, young daughters [to] produce a society of . . . welfare recipient mongrels," thereby turning America's cities into "jungles." A local reporter caught wind of the message, but John Howard denied any involvement and began referring all calls to a spokesperson.

That spokesperson turned out to be Barry Black, Howard's Pennsylvania-based Imperial Wizard. As spokespersons go, he was an odd choice—Black had been even more antagonistic with the press than Howard. Not long after the shop opened, for example, he had promised to pull the Klan out of Laurens entirely—so long as residents banded together and purchased the Echo for "a million dollars." With Black at the helm, the Redneck Shop's public image would only get worse. In an interview with *Vibe* magazine, he boasted about a recent acquisition at the shop, an old black-and-white photo from 1913. "It was a black person hung for raping a white woman," he said. "That picture's worth—in a Klansman's eyes—$1,000. We'll probably have copies made and sell them at the store for $5 apiece. Maybe make postcards out of them."

He was talking, of course, about the photo of Richard Puckett—the same photo Rev. Kennedy had used in his protests. And the postcards (unlike his pledge to leave Laurens) were a promise Black made good on. By summer, reprints were available for sale, and sometimes given away as a "free gift with purchase." Black could hardly claim credit for the idea, however. Commemorative photographs and picture postcards of lynchings had been extraordinarily common in the early part of the twentieth century, sold as souvenirs and sent through the mail as casually and as frequently as greeting cards. Black was merely resurrecting one of the ugliest (and most effective) forms of white supremacist intimidation.

And still the customers came.

Teddy Craine of Enoree stopped in to buy a T-shirt for his four-year-old son. "This is part of my past," he explained to the *Greenville News*. "My great-grandfather fought for the Confederacy. The United States stands up for people's rights. That is why we are here today. I don't think our heritage should be put in a back room."

Roger Stow, a carpenter from Greenville, bought a Klan cap. "I see nothing wrong with selling Klan stuff because it is part of our proud heritage, whether blacks and white liberals like it or not."

Stephanie Wilke, twenty-two, told the *Washington Post* that she had no qualms about supporting the Klan or asserting her rights as a white person. "The blacks wear Malcolm X T-shirts," she said. "These words are our heritage. It's the South, it's the rebel flag."

Would they have continued patronizing the shop had they known what Mike Burden was up to?

Ed McDaniel might have been a nuisance, but his activism against the shop had been relatively tame. Rev. Kennedy, with his advocacy in the statehouse and warnings of an imminent race war, was far more dangerous. Or at least that's what Burden came to believe. The day Hunter plowed his van into the shop, for example, mere hours after Burden had finished boarding up the windows, a sudden earsplitting crack—like the sound of a gunshot—sent nearly everyone inside diving for cover. It turned out not to have been a gun at all, luckily, just the sound of a fishing reel slamming into the boards, tossed at the shop by a group of mischievous kids. But the incident left everyone a bit shaken. And Howard had been quick to lay the blame at Rev. Kennedy's feet, suggesting over and over again that the reverend was responsible for the escalation, that tensions were bound to get worse, that next time it really would be a gun.

"We were told more or less that our lives were gonna be . . . taken care of," Burden said later. So when John gave him a new assignment, he took the job very seriously. For the next several weeks, when Burden wasn't at the shop or spending time with Judy, he was doing reconnaissance on the reverend—trailing him around town, watching, waiting. "I knew where he lived," he says of Kennedy. "I knew where he worked. I knew where he went. I knew what stores he liked, his favorite restaurant . . ." At some point Burden considered driving to a secluded spot on Kennedy's regular route and faking car trouble, figuring that a reverend would surely pull over in order to help a stranded motorist. There would be no witnesses, as he later explained in interviews with *The State*, and the attack would look like a robbery.

"The Klan has a saying," Burden explained. "It's *Non silba sed anthar*. 'Not for self, but for others.'" The motto is a mix of Latin and Gothic, a holdover from the second Ku Klux Klan of the early twentieth century, and it had been drilled into him since his earliest days with John Howard. Why do Klansmen take security at rallies and other events so seriously? *Non silba sed anthar*—to protect their brothers in arms. Why was the Klan's mission so important? *Non silba sed anthar*—it was in the service of the white race. Burden and his fellow Klansmen spoke the words often, almost like a passcode or private greeting. A little placard bearing the motto was tacked up next to the register in the Redneck Shop. And in Burden's mind, stalking the reverend was just another way that he was putting the safety of his adopted family before his own needs. It was about defense and protection. It was honorable.

In the days leading up to his second major rally, Rev. Kennedy led his church in a frenzy of activities: prayer vigils, community meetings, a silent ride through the center of town, and a bonfire gathering at New Beginning, all intended to raise awareness and encourage community participation. By Saturday morning, however, it was clear that his movement was losing ground. Just six weeks earlier, four hundred people had packed the square at his invitation. Now he was looking at a crowd of about fifty—a good third of whom weren't protesters at all, but rather law enforcement officers and members of the media.

"We could have had others come," he told reporters, putting a spin on the disappointing turnout, "but we wanted to mentally prepare our people that there will be times when only a handful will be there to carry the load. It's going to be a long, hot summer. We will not be intimidated."

With characteristic brashness, Kennedy blasted community leaders for not having done enough to address the Redneck Shop, and went so far as to call Governor Beasley a "liar" for suggesting that race relations in South Carolina were "good." He threatened to bring his protests to the door of the statehouse, called for the NAACP and the Southern Christian Leadership Conference to join the fight, pleaded for more and stronger support from white citizens. "We can't solve the problem with one race," he said.

But the plea wasn't working. Local business owners were already tired of the disruption from so many protests. They didn't care for Kennedy's style, nor see much point in his antagonism—

the shop wasn't going anywhere. More than a few blamed him, publicly, for "blowing things out of proportion." There was one person, however, with whom Kennedy was not losing momentum, but rather gaining ground. That was Judy.

At first, she had been plenty suspicious of Rev. Kennedy. She'd heard an earful from Mike and John, after all: that the reverend was supposedly behind the instances of random vandalism at the shop, that he was goading blacks into violence and jeopardizing her boyfriend's livelihood. After she'd gotten a glimpse into the inner workings of the Klan, however, she hadn't exactly been impressed with John Howard, either. Judy had always been told that she was part Cherokee, so when the inevitable chatter about the inferiority of nonwhites came up— when Howard launched into one of his tirades about the blacks or the Mexicans or the Chinese—she decided to confront him. "If you're gonna hate the blacks because of the color of their skin, then why do you want *me* to be in the Klan?" she asked. "I come from Indian. You hate me 'cause I got Indian in me?"

Whatever his true feelings, John neglected to share them. "He couldn't give me an answer," Judy says. "So I thought, 'Mm-hmm. *Okay.*'" In the meantime, she continued to push Mike. "I would challenge him, you know? 'All right, I went to a Klan meeting. Now let's go do my thing.'" Usually that meant driving out to KC's, a run-down honky-tonk out on Highway 221, to hear her favorite band play. And for a brief period, she seemed to be winning Burden over—they went out together, away from the Klan, nearly every weekend. But then some new "job" would come up, some new errand Mike was supposed to run for John, some new mission to fulfill. "I would tell her, it's my *duty,*" Mike said later. "I've got to do this."

By the time she found out that Mike was essentially stalking the reverend, Judy was desperate. She had long since stopped going to meetings, socialized less and less with the few female members she'd gotten to know during initiation. And when she wandered into the courthouse square during Kennedy's second rally, something clicked. "I was like, 'This makes sense now,'" Judy explained. "*Now* I understand why John Howard doesn't like him." The more she listened to the reverend's calls for non-violent protest, for a coming together of the races, the more she understood that her boyfriend was on the wrong side. "I kinda understood where Reverend Kennedy was coming from," she says. "And I thought, 'You know, that's right. What he's sayin is right.'"

A DAY OR two later, Rev. Kennedy met with more disgruntled churchgoers—this time a young African American couple. "I know what you're getting ready to say," Kennedy told them, having at that point counseled quite a few young people who'd come by to discuss the relative merits of just blowing the place up. This couple was different. They were headed to the square, they said, where they intended to take care of the problem themselves—no more protests.

"I said, 'Give me your word that you ain't gonna do nuthin like that,'" Kennedy remembers. He told them he was tired and frustrated, just as they were, but violence would only make things worse. He gave his standard exhortation about fighting back peacefully—he told them they couldn't lower themselves to John Howard's level, couldn't mimic the Klan's ideology and forsake the teachings of the Bible. But as he watched the man and woman climb into their car and drive away from the church, Kennedy figured he'd best follow them over there. "Sometimes when you fed up like that, when you *tired...*," Kennedy said, shaking his head. This time, he feared, his words might not have done very much good.

It was dusk by the time he pulled into one of the parking spaces on the north side of the courthouse. The streetlamps had come on, and the lights from inside the shop cast an orange glow across the whole of West Laurens Street. The couple, as promised, was outside raising hell, shouting epithets in the direction of the store and calling for the Klansmen to come out. Kennedy quickened his pace just in time to see John Howard step out onto one of the twin fire escapes above the marquee. He hadn't, however, seen what happened seconds earlier: John hollering at Mike to get upstairs, and Mike, armed with a Makarov .380 pistol and a .22 in his pocket, ascending to the roof.

Kennedy had almost closed the gap between himself and the couple, trying to conjure some strategy to defuse the situation, when he heard Howard suddenly call down to him. For all the time they had spent trading barbs in the press, it was the first time either man had ever spoken to the other. Full of false bonhomie, in a kind of singsongy lilt, Howard invited the reverend to come on inside. He suggested Kennedy might like to have his picture taken while wearing a Klansman's robe.

One floor above, Mike was crouched behind the redbrick parapet at the front of the roof. Down and to the right, he could see the top of Howard's head, or at any rate the top of the Confederate-flag ball cap John usually wore to cover his bald spot. Mike curled his finger around the trigger and sat at attention, waiting for a sign or a signal. "I didn't care about the consequences," he said. "I will defend what's mine at all costs. I had the shot lined up and everything. I had him in my sights."

Down on street level, Kennedy had the distinct impression

that he was being goaded, that Howard was trying to provoke him into a more direct confrontation, a feeling with which he was not entirely unfamiliar. *"Any* kind of reaction from a black man is a sin," he said. "You can't be reactionary to them. You have to make them react to you. This is the thing about fighting back—I even tell my kids this. There are reprisals, there are consequences whenever you take a stand, but the consequences are worse when you're black. Because in their minds, the nigger oughta be in his place." Instead of engaging with Howard, then, Kennedy focused on the couple. And instead of reiterating the conciliatory message he'd given in his office—since it hadn't worked the first time—he took on the persona of a football coach giving a pre-game pep talk. "I'm gonna stick 'em with protests!" he shouted, pointing at the shop. "Back to back! We will not be intimidated! You intimidated?"

The couple exchanged glances. "No."

"I said, *you intimidated?*"

"No!"

From his perch on the roof, Mike felt something akin to confusion. For weeks, he'd anticipated some kind of covert attack. He had followed Kennedy back and forth across town, trying to glean some insight into his plans, collecting intel on the man he considered the greatest threat to his shop and his person. But Kennedy, loud as he may have been—he was shouting about protesting and leading call-and-response chants and singing that ridiculous pump-it-up song—was actually moving the protesters away from the building. "He was down there sayin, 'Y'all need to back up. This is the wrong way to do it. We can protest peacefully,' stuff like that," Burden recalled. "I think that was mainly the reason I didn't fulfill the mission. He was no longer a threat."

. . .

LATER THAT NIGHT, Burden arrived at Judy's trailer with a kind of sheepish grin on his face. He paced back and forth in her tiny kitchen, then finally plopped onto the sofa and put his head in his hands. "You'll never guess what I almost done."

Judy sighed. "What have you almost done *now?*"

By then, Judy was well aware of Burden's unnaturally close relationship with John Howard. She'd seen the way Mike seemed to hang on John's every word; in fact, she was convinced that Mike was afraid to defy him. She knew, too, about the abuse Mike had suffered as a child. She knew that John had taken Mike in when he had nowhere else to go. But it wasn't until Mike began to tell her about aiming a gun at the reverend that she understood how deep it all went.

"What are you doin this for?" she said. "Because John Howard can't stand to be around him? You're gonna give up your whole life—and me and these kids. You're gonna go to prison for the rest of your life. Do you think John Howard is going to be there for you then?"

The more she pushed, the quieter Mike got—a personality trait to which she had long since grown accustomed. "When Mike gets real quiet and just sets there and looks at you? He doesn't want to talk about it anymore, 'cause you done hit a nerve." Finally, she scooted over to him and put a hand on his knee. "Listen, I love you," she said, "but you have got to break away from this."

Mike was not yet ready to renounce John Howard, but there was no denying that things were different now. He was no longer an orphan with nothing to lose. He suddenly had people who loved him—*really* loved him, without asking for anything in return. The sudden vulnerability was no less than terrifying. In love letters to Judy, written in small, blocky script and decorated with hearts and flowers, he poured out the emotions that he struggled to express in person. "The feelings that are with me do scare the hell out of me," he wrote. "I'm supposed to be as strong as a rock, now this rock is crumbling." Just a few months ago, he would have lashed out at anyone who dared challenge him or the Klan. Now he had to wonder if that sacrifice was worth it.

"I think he was coming to me to talk it through," Judy said later. "You know, 'This is what I done. Is this right or is it wrong?' I mean, he couldn't even think for his own self. John had him so brainwashed."

From then on, she worked to replace John in that capacity. She struck up conversations challenging Mike's ideology, and she started imagining for them both a different kind of life. Mike had talked idly about wanting to be a truck driver—some distant uncle had apparently been trucking for years—and it seemed like a good fit for him. He didn't feel particularly comfortable cooped up inside or working in a factory, and anyway, there wasn't even much factory work left in Laurens. A trucker's salary might provide real financial stability; as it was, Judy was teetering on the brink of eviction. She just had to get Mike away from the Klan, and away from John Howard. Maybe away from Laurens altogether. "I kept pressuring him," she said. "Let's walk away from it. Let's get out of it."

Little by little, it seemed to be working. "I had nothin in the world before I met Judy," Burden says. "I had *nothing*. I didn't have no cares. I didn't care about anybody's feelings. I was a very angry person. But Judy once told somebody that she saw a side of me nobody else seen. She was what made me think.

Because I was a soldier. I mean, I do what I'm told and drive on. But her, she would make me sit down and we'd talk and it'd be like, 'Well, you're right. You've got a point there.' She was my conscience."

One night that spring, Judy and Mike went back to the bar on Highway 221 to hear the same band play—the White Buffalo Band, a Greenwood-based southern rock cover band. Mike had gotten friendly with some of the members. "I went up, talked to that lead singer, told 'em what I was gonna do," he said. "Grabbed that wireless mic . . ."

Over at the bar, Judy turned around and realized she had no idea where her boyfriend was. "All of a sudden, he disappears." She swiveled in her chair and hopped off her stool. Then suddenly she heard his voice come through over the loudspeaker.

"Judy, I love you. Will you marry me?"

Mike had climbed up onstage and dropped down on one knee. Whoops and cheers rang out from the crowd. "I was in love with him," Judy said later. "And I thought, 'Well, he really loves me and my kids. He'll go along. He'll shy away from the Klan.' For a while there, I thought he had." So she said yes.

six

"CHOOSE"

Despite her loose affiliation with the Redneck Shop and her relationship with Mike Burden, Judy was kept mostly in the dark when it came to the inner workings of the Keystone Knights of the Ku Klux Klan. She'd never been privy to high-level talks or strategy sessions, and she had only a cursory knowledge of the various dignitaries who stopped by with increasing frequency, whether to inspect the merchandise, drop off application forms and white supremacist literature, or inquire about renting out the meeting hall. As for John Howard's plans, all she knew was that he'd hired a lawyer at some point. "They kept that private," she said. The phone would ring; John would summon Mike to a room in the back of the shop and ask his wife, Hazel, to take over the register for a spell.

By early May, just days after Mike and Judy were married at the courthouse in a no-frills civil ceremony, everyone in Laurens found out what those clandestine conversations had been about: John Howard was suing Councilman Ed McDaniel for slander. The lawsuit, filed on Howard's behalf with the Laurens county clerk's office, cited McDaniel's comments to the press, suggesting that Howard might have been involved in the van incident. The suit alleged that McDaniel had tarnished Howard's reputation in an attempt to "curry political favor." In the filing, the Redneck Shop's proprietor was cast as an upstanding, law-abiding citizen, one who had never been charged with any crime of "moral turpitude." (Perhaps his 1970 arrest on suspicion of murder had been expunged from the record.)

For his part, McDaniel didn't seem particularly worried. "I would not spend 15 cents on an attorney to defend this," he told the *Clinton Chronicle*. Still, the suit was a clear sign that Howard had no intention of backing down. He had also started speaking out against his *other* nemesis—by name this time. "If Mr. Kennedy wants to continue [with his protests]," he told a group of reporters, "he's going to end up in trouble. I'm just interested in putting a stop to all this foolishness taking place."

McDaniel and Kennedy were far from the only folks with whom Howard was fighting, however. Because now he had to contend with Judy, too.

Even before their marriage, Judy had set about trying to discredit John Howard in the eyes of her husband. Seemingly every chance she got, Judy would goad Howard into an argument—about race, about prejudice, about southern history, about the Klan. "I'd sit back and I'd actually think of stuff to argue about," she said, "and then when Mike and I would leave, I would be like, 'See how ignorant he really is?'" After their marriage, her influence on Burden had only grown. Mike had officially moved into her trailer; for the first time in seven years, he wasn't living on the Lanford property, wasn't at Howard's constant beck and call. And the more time he spent with his wife and stepchildren, the more receptive he became to Judy's insistence that the Redneck Shop had caused them all nothing but problems.

In late May, yet another scuffle broke out on the square. This time a white male in his mid-twenties, Herbert Neely, wandered inside the Redneck Shop and began tearing down the makeshift curtains tacked up along the front windows to block the sunlight. John Howard promptly called the police, though Neely wandered right back out of the store only moments later, as wordlessly as he'd arrived. By the time Lieutenant P. J. Quinton showed up to take Howard's statement, Wild Bill was rushing in—he'd heard about the disturbance and intended to help out his friend. In his hand was a sawed-off pump-action shotgun with a pistol grip—illegal in the state of South Carolina. Hoff spent the evening in jail. Bond was set for $30,000.

Each new drama or showdown at the store seemed only to confirm what Judy had been telling him. And for a few weeks that spring and summer, the Burdens enjoyed something close to a happy, somewhat stress-free life. Then they got served with eviction papers.

"I got behind in the rent," Judy said, "and Mike wasn't really workin. . . ." That she'd been expecting the eviction notice did not in any way lessen the blow—she had no savings and no safety net, and in seven days they had to be out.

"I was graspin at straws," she says. "You know, 'How are we gonna get the money? What are we gonna do?' And Mike said, 'There's only one person I can turn to.'"

He had gone to John Howard in the hope of securing a loan or an advance on his earnings in order to make a down payment on a trailer. Howard, however, wasn't willing to offer any financial assistance. Instead, he offered the Burdens a place to stay: the "apartment" in the basement of the Redneck Shop.

The arrangement was supposed to be temporary—and it's not as though Judy had any other options. But whatever she imagined, whatever reservations she had, the reality turned out to be far worse. For all the attention paid to renovating the Echo's street-level space, virtually nothing had been done to the basement. It was damp, musty, dark, sectioned off into what passed for three different "rooms"—a living area, a bedroom, and a makeshift "washroom," little more than a garden tub hauled into a corner, to which you could run water via a hose. No toilet. The tiny amount of light filtering through the garden-level windows did little more than illuminate a blanket of dust. "You couldn't breathe in there," Judy said. "It was a nightmare."

The state of the accommodations was one thing; the sudden proximity of her children to the Klan—or of the Klan to her children—was another thing entirely.

In the earliest days of her flirtation with Mike, long before Judy attended a meeting or learned the truth about the Klan, she had brought her children, Brian and Stacy, along on visits to the Lanford property and to the Redneck Shop in order to check out the renovations in progress. That in itself was not unusual—both the shop and John Howard's property were usually crawling with children. "If you're a Klan member, your kids are there," Stacy said years later. "And the kids are basically absorbing any- and everything that's talked about." She was a few months shy of her eleventh birthday then: blond, bespectacled, a bit of an introvert, but also very smart, with a wry sense of humor. For the most part she liked Mike—though she was a bit suspicious of the speed at which he'd seemingly replaced her father—but it hadn't taken her long to determine that she was no fan of John Howard. "He'd be like, 'Don't you wanna grow up to be like us?'" she remembers. "He had my friend Katie totally convinced—at eight years old—that we needed to start a junior Klan chapter."

Whatever John Howard was selling, ten-year-old Stacy wasn't buying it.

Even worse, in her eyes, was Wild Bill Hoff. Ever since arriving in South Carolina sometime in the early 1990s, Wild Bill's primary place of residence had been the Lanford property. As renovations on the shop got further under way, however, he began spending an increasing amount of time in a makeshift apartment on the second floor of the Echo theater. He largely kept to himself, but one day he offered to give Stacy guitar lessons.

"I really wanted to learn how to play," she said, "but he had a creepy vibe to him. And he would never come downstairs. He would always want me to go upstairs in his room." Nothing untoward ever happened, but there was no doubt that Bill made her uncomfortable. Judy, meanwhile, had known virtually nothing about Wild Bill's criminal past, but the mere hint that something inappropriate might have gone on upstairs brought out the fire in her. "I'd *kill* him."

Judy and her family moved into the basement sometime in mid-June, but she kept virtually all of their belongings boxed up, pulling out only what she needed to get through the day— she had no intention of staying long. And when it came to her children, she was emphatic about keeping her eyes on them. "I kept 'em right here with me," she said. "So I could see 'em and I'd know what was going on around 'em at all times. I told 'em, you stay right here with me. You don't have anything to say to *none* of 'em."

Meanwhile, tensions between her and John Howard continued to escalate. "We would go out and buy food for the month," Stacy explained, "and of course we was on food stamps. But John would let his employees come down there and eat everything."

When Judy broached the subject with her husband, it seemed like he was in denial. "Well, you livin here for free. What did you expect?" he said. "You gonna say something just because one of the guys ate a snack cake?"

It was around that time that she discovered, buried among her son's possessions, a small pocketknife bearing the Klan's logo.

"I asked Brian where he got it," she recalled. "And he said, 'John Howard gave it to me. He told me I could be a future Klansman.'"

She took it from him, of course, but it was just further confirmation that the situation she was in wasn't just an inconvenience or a temporary rough patch. It was dangerous.

THE FARMING COMMUNITY of Pelion—population five hundred—sits little more than an hour's drive southeast of Laurens, nestled among dense pine forests just west of Columbia. It was originally a whistle-stop, one of several small towns that sprang up along the old Carolina Midland Railway around the turn of the century. In more recent times, Pelion has become known for its annual Peanut Party, a two-day autumn festival honoring the region's most cherished crop. But for more than thirty years, the town was also home to one of the state's most notorious residents—and John Howard's friend—Grand Dragon of the Christian Knights of the Ku Klux Klan, Horace King.

King was born two counties over in 1933, the son of a poor sharecropper, one of ten children expected to work the fields rather than attend school with any regularity. "Nobody could have been brought up worse than I was," he once told a reporter from the Orangeburg *Times and Democrat.* "Part of the time we didn't have nuthin to eat. We were in the fields from sunup to after sundown." He dropped out by the sixth grade, and for the rest of his life remained functionally illiterate.

It was a hard life, and the years of privation showed. At sixty-three, King could easily have passed for two *decades* older. He was tall and gaunt, with extreme, almost witchlike features: deep-set eyes, sharp cheekbones, a pointed chin. His bottom lip rolled permanently inward, probably a side effect of a lifelong tobacco habit.

Like John Howard, King found a sense of purpose with the United Klans of America during the turmoil of the civil rights movement. He gradually moved up the ranks until 1985, when he broke away and helped to form the Christian Knights. At around the same time, he also purchased (with money he'd collected from his followers) a seven-acre plot off an unpaved, red-clay road, which served as both his home and a headquarters for Klan activity in the state.

The house was a simple frame affair, yellow shiplap with a gray shingled roof. A single-story outbuilding fifty yards to the northeast doubled as a meeting hall. But during rallies—such as the one held on June 29, 1996—the flat field between the buildings transformed. A folding card table became a makeshift concession stand; a tent canopy housed the various knickknacks for sale (T-shirts, pocketknives, and all manner of trinkets bearing the Klan logo). A wooden utility trailer was trucked in to serve as a mobile pulpit. King, dressed in his knee-length satin robe, presided from the stage. "A race war is coming!" he hollered. "The Klan is the only hope for the white race!"

King was known for his fiery rhetoric, and his speeches always revolved around the same themes: that black people were lazy and government-dependent ("the taxpayers in the South is what's feeding them bums you see laying in the street"), that black churches were evil, and that it was up to white folks to beat or burn or otherwise drive them out. In fact, virtually nothing about the June rally was different from any other held in the previous twenty or thirty years—the same soundtrack crackled from ancient speakers ("The Old Rugged Cross" and other gospel songs). The same jury-rigged pews—planks of wood set atop five-gallon drums—formed a semicircle around the stage. The same sweet stink of kerosene wafted through the air.

There was, however, one small addition to the proceedings that evening. An upturned ball cap—a makeshift collection plate—was circulating among the crowd. King was raising money for a legal defense fund, after being served with a lawsuit that all but threatened to end the Christian Knights.

Over the previous few months, concerns about the wave of church fires across the region had only grown more intense. For the Christian Knights, however, the situation was suddenly dire. Two of King's acolytes, Timothy Welch and Gary Christopher Cox, had been arrested for the back-to-back burnings of two rural churches in nearby Manning, South Carolina. Now one of those churches, Macedonia Baptist, was suing the Christian Knights—and Horace King, specifically—for using "disparaging and inflammatory statements about black churches" to inspire and encourage the burnings. The lead attorney was Morris Dees, co-founder of the Southern Poverty Law Center, the same Morris Dees who had effectively bankrupted Robert Shelton's UKA and J. W. Farrands's Invisible Empire.

"This is a conspiracy," King thundered from the stage, "but it's a conspiracy against the white race. The Klan is not about race hatred. It's about the Bible."

Considering the seriousness of the charges—not to mention

the size of the SPLC's endowment, some $68 million—King's backyard rally was unlikely to put much of a dent in his Klan faction's mounting legal fees. But to the men gathered that night, it was an issue of honor. Virgil Griffin had driven down from North Carolina to mark the occasion, shoving a few crumpled dollar bills into the impromptu collection plate. "I will not bow to Morris Dees," he said. "The only way he's going to stop me is to kill me."

Interestingly, the biggest donation of the night didn't come from a member of the Christian Knights at all. It came from Howard's old friend and accomplice Barry Black, who had pledged the Keystone Knights' loyalty and support in fighting the suit. "We haven't done anything to deserve this persecution," he said, dropping $50 into the hat. Representatives of the Christian Identity movement and the Aryan Nation had made the trek to rural Lexington County, too. The mingling among usually disparate groups had put law enforcement officials and Klan watchers on edge.

"It's a concern," Chief Robert Stewart of the State Law Enforcement Division told the Associated Press. Jack Levin, director for the study of violence and social conflict at Northeastern University and a well-known expert on hate crimes, also expressed dismay. Increasingly, he noted, the Klan and its allies were relying on Christianity to "lend an air of religious credibility" to their message and drive recruitment.

Of particular interest was a twenty-six-page pamphlet, *The Bible Answers Racial Questions*, which purported to show biblical "evidence" supporting segregation. Passages were quoted out of context, alongside analysis that described black people as "cursed," exalted white people as "chosen," and—most troubling, given the circumstances—advocated the burning of black churches (e.g., "But ye shall destroy their altars, break down their images, and cut down their groves"; Exodus 34:13). The booklet, blue-jacketed and crudely stapled, had surfaced at King's late June rally, a development that received considerable press attention. No one, however, seemed to have any clue as to its origins.

In fact, it was written in the mid-1950s by an Alabaman named Eugene S. Hall. At the time, Hall was a fairly prominent member of Montgomery society and a director of his local White Citizens Council, though he caused a bit of a stir by staging a mock hanging at the courthouse square during the Montgomery bus boycott. Rosa Parks had been arrested just six months earlier, and the demonstration was intended as a show of force. Law enforcement would have done well to take him seriously. Less than a year later, Hall was arrested along with six other men in connection with a wave of bombings across the city. Targets included four African American churches and the homes of three African American ministers, including Martin Luther King Jr.

All seven co-conspirators were acquitted, however, and Hall's racism never abated. By the mid-'70s he was cavorting with James Venable and the National Knights in Stone Mountain, Georgia. "Took me years to do that book," he told journalist Patsy Sims, before launching into a bizarre screed about the inferiority of blacks and the biological differences between the races. When asked about his religious background, Hall readily admitted that he was self-taught. Despite his lack of formal education and training—despite an appallingly poor grasp of Christian theology—Hall's pamphlet achieved a fairly impressive reach in the decades that followed. In 1974, the booklet turned up in the mailbox of a federal judge, W. Arthur Garrity, after his ruling in *Morgan v. Hennigan* led to the compulsory busing of students in Boston's public school system. By the 1980s *The Bible Answers Racial Questions* was circulating among members of the Christian Identity movement, and at some point in the 1990s it was available for sale from an Aryan Nations catalog based out of Idaho. Its sudden presence in South Carolina, however, suggested a potential link between the book and the church fires.

"I would like to get my hands on it," Chief Stewart admitted when questioned by reporters.

Had he been so inclined, he could have easily found a copy at the Redneck Shop. A month or so before the Pelion rally, a Laurens resident was presented with the booklet and a membership application to the Klan by none other than John Howard. When reached by a local reporter for comment, Howard explained that the booklet had merely been left at the shop "by the International Keystone Knights"—an odd way of denying culpability, since he was a high-ranking member of the same organization—then grew flustered, claimed he was being harassed, and hung up the phone.

It was exactly the kind of thing Rev. Kennedy had worried about. Far from being a simple southern pride store, the Redneck Shop had become a Klan crossroads, a meeting place for high-level members to strategize and hold sway over young and impressionable recruits. The shop's proximity to the courthouse, and the fact that it was housed in a historic building, added yet another layer of legitimacy.

By summer, the Keystone Knights had finished renovating the old screening room at the back of the theater. A giant mural of a hooded Klansman on horseback was painted on the back wall. A stage had been erected, on top of which stood a lectern, the lightbulb-studded cross from Plantation Concrete, and an array of flags.

"That's where they had the podium and stuff set up," Stacy explained.

Not that the children were permitted to spend much time there. Various Klan factions—in addition to Howard's Keystone Klan—had been granted permission to hold their klavern meetings in the projection room, but Howard didn't want Judy or her kids near the action. During the day, he told them to enter and exit through the rear of the building, and when Howard locked up the shop for the night, he insisted that the family stay down in the basement, so as not to trigger the security alarms.

Within a matter of days, the situation had become untenable. At Judy's urging, Burden again asked Howard for financial help. It seemed like a fairly reasonable request; Burden had worked for John for seven years, hardly asking for anything. Again, however, Howard turned him down. More than that, he suggested that Judy wasn't worth the effort. "He could see she was becoming an influence on me," Burden says. "So he more or less wanted to get her away from me." Howard started to make accusations—that Judy wasn't good for Mike, that she didn't really care about him. For perhaps the first time in his life, Burden put Howard in check. "You need to back off and leave me the hell alone," he told him. "This is *my* family, not yours."

Burden didn't think the fight was all that consequential. He and Howard had bickered before, without incident. It wasn't until several days later that he realized this fight had been different.

A WEEK AFTER the rally in Pelion, Judy was no more settled into her new, if ostensibly temporary, home. In the damp of the basement, the temperature soared past 100 degrees. The dust made it difficult to breathe. She had to get out.

"It was the Fourth of July," she said, "and I couldn't take my kids on vacation like a normal family would do." Instead, she bought supplies for a simple picnic lunch—sandwich meat, chips, drinks. "I said, 'We'll go down to the river, just to let 'em get out and have a . . . you know, a *break* from that place.'"

The Enoree River flows southeastward for eighty-five miles across the upper piedmont, joining up with the Broad River just south of Clinton. It's a popular canoeing destination in the late spring and early fall, when the rains cause the river to swell, but in summer months, the Enoree shrinks to something more like a creek, hemmed in by floodplain forests and hardwood bluffs. It is totally isolated—peaceful, quiet.

Judy, Mike, and the kids spent the afternoon lolling along the shoreline a few miles outside town. "The kids played, we ate lunch," Judy said. It was evening by the time they drove back to town and Mike pulled the family's truck into the parking lot on the west side of the shop. He left Judy behind to rouse the kids—half asleep, faces flushed from a day in the sun—trudged down the little embankment at the rear of the shop, walked up the ramp, and reached for the door. It wouldn't budge.

"What do you mean, 'locked out'?" Judy asked, incredulous.

Mike explained about the fight, about how he'd gotten up the nerve to ask for some help, about how John had rebuffed him. Judy had clearly been right about John; now, as some kind of retaliation, they'd been locked out of the only home they could afford. The speed with which it all came crashing down was perhaps the only truly surprising part. The realization of how dire the situation was, however, was slower to come.

"Keep in mind," he said later, "everything we own is in there. All we've got is what we've got on our back and what we got in the pickup truck."

That was putting it mildly. They had no money. The rest

of Judy's groceries—purchased with food stamps—were locked inside, too. They had nowhere to sleep until this mess got sorted out, save for the truck. Judy was livid.

"Choose," she said. "Right here, right now."

Burden stared at her blankly.

"I'm done. You choose *this*," she said, gesturing to the shop, "or me and my kids. I'm not putting my kids through this no more. I'm out of here. I'm gone."

Burden looked back at the shop. For the last five years, his entire life, his entire identity, had revolved around that building. He had considered it a sort of retirement plan, a safety net. It was his only real asset in the world. But suddenly it represented something entirely different: a lie. Everything John had ever told him about the Klan—the boasts about protecting women and children, the stories about the charitable donations and the sense of fraternity and family—all of it rang hollow now that he'd been turned out.

He didn't have to choose. The choice was made for him.

They spent the night in Burden's truck, Stacy and Brian stretched out in the bed, Judy curled against Mike's chest in the front seat. But Mike didn't sleep. He seethed.

"I was like, 'This is bullshit,'" he said. Two young Klansmen were sitting in a jail in Clarendon County at that very moment. Their leader, Horace King, had cut them loose, claiming that he didn't even really *know* them. It didn't take a rocket scientist to figure out what Howard would have done had Burden gone through with any of his plots against Rev. Kennedy.

He realized there was only one way to get back at Howard.

"People in Laurens tried everything in the world to shut that business down," he said. "They couldn't do it, because I'd had the business license prior to the actual store being revealed. I mean, everybody *knew* what it was. But until the city seen it, they couldn't do anything about it."

More than anyone else save John Howard, Burden also knew the shortcuts they had taken to secure that license—hiding issues with the wiring, camouflaging parts of the building that weren't up to code. By dawn, he'd made his decision. "That's when I done the 'I'll show you.'"

Shortly after eight on Monday morning, Mike Burden marched through the front door of City Hall and surrendered the Redneck Shop's business license.

seven

"THIS NEW BEGINNING, AIN'T IT?"

For Reverend Kennedy, the morning of Monday, July 8, had begun like any other. The pastor let himself in through the church's side door, the smells of his aunt Alberta's cooking already wafting from the Soup Kitchen to the sanctuary— collards, okra, onions frying in butter.

In the office, he found his assistant, Frances, fielding phone calls and arranging stacks of real estate paperwork atop his desk. New Beginning was preparing to purchase twenty-eight acres off the Highway 127 bypass, where Kennedy would fulfill his longtime dream of building a community center—a multi-cultural center, as he'd taken to calling it. The finished complex was to have a daycare center and a senior citizens' program, a storage room for the donated clothes now piled high in the empty front office of his church, a mess hall to house the Soup Kitchen, a library, an after-school tutoring program, a health clinic, and acres of athletic fields. It was a wildly ambitious project—perhaps too ambitious. The only thing not settled was the question of money. To that end, Kennedy was launching a letter-writing program and putting out a call to sign up as many volunteer laborers as possible. He planned to reach out to state and local politicians, too—even Governor Beasley himself. If the governor wanted to insist that race relations in South Carolina were *good*, Kennedy figured, let him put his money where his mouth is.

Every few minutes throughout the course of that morning, Frances popped in to announce the arrival of yet another parishioner awaiting an audience with the reverend. A factory was threatening to close its doors and ship its jobs to Mexico. A jailer on medical leave had received a subpar evaluation after her testimony in a court case led to a dismissal of the charges. By late morning, a line of folks snaked along the hallway and straight out the door. Amid the chaos, Frances handed Kennedy the phone—a parishioner was calling from the local police department. "Somebody had a situation with the law," Kennedy remembers. "So I had gone over to talk to the chief about something."

Kennedy's trip to the police station turned out to be a quick errand; it was still shy of noon by the time he set out across the parking lot toward his vehicle. By then, the temperature had soared to ninety degrees. The air above the asphalt was hazy with heat, and Kennedy could feel his dress shirt turning wet at the back. He was pulling his keys from his pocket, lost in thought, when he heard someone call out to him.

"Could you help me out?"

The man, slouched against the hood of a pickup truck, was rail-thin. Dirt was caked on the knees of his jeans. Rev. Kennedy counted at least three visible tattoos—most notably, on the man's right biceps, a figure on horseback waving a scythe in front of a billowing Confederate flag. Though they had never met before, Kennedy recognized Michael Burden immediately. "I knew he was part of the shop," he said later. "I knew he was a Klansman."

Kennedy's eyes swept past Burden to the truck and the little family assembled inside it. "I looked at *them* and I thought, 'Lord have mercy.'"

He could see two little faces peeking out from below the truck's camper shell, both flushed red from the heat, hair wet and glistening at the temples. The girl, who looked to be about ten, had a mop of dirty-blond ringlets and a sheepishness about her, all hunched shoulders and downcast eyes. The boy was older, with dark brown hair and the wispy beginnings of a mustache shadowing his upper lip. On the far side of the truck, loitering near the open passenger door, was a petite woman, hair dyed a brassy blond, styled in a kind of teased-out bouffant straight out of the 1980s. She had on a loose-fitting crop top and athletic shorts. She was so skinny. They were all so skinny. Kennedy wondered how long they'd been living in that truck— and why no one else seemed to be helping them.

"Have those children eaten today?" Kennedy said.

"No, sir." Burden bowed his head. "I know you may not like me, but my wife and these young'uns . . ."

The reverend silenced him with a flick of the wrist. "We can talk about our differences later," he said. He took a few steps toward his car, turned, and waved. "Well? Y'all follow me."

It was a three-minute drive from the Laurens police station to the redbrick church, a straight shot down East Main. Burden pulled his truck into a space out front and reluctantly followed Kennedy in through the church's side door.

"This my sister Pam," Kennedy said to the Burdens, gesturing to a pretty middle-aged woman standing in the hallway outside his office. "And this Frances." To Pam and Frances he said, "These folks are here from the Redneck Shop."

Judy looked at Pam and Frances, well dressed and conservative, and then down at her own clothes, suddenly self-conscious. "I was in a pair of shorts, flip-flops, and a top about up to here," she says. "Mike had a T-shirt and jeans on. And they kinda looked at us like, 'Are you serious?'"

Before anyone was forced to make small talk, Kennedy came back with a small wad of cash and a set of instructions: "We'll find you somewhere to stay tonight. Go get you a change of clothes, toiletries, whatever you need. Toothbrush, soap. Don't be ashamed about getting it. Just get what you need. Get yourselves freshened up and meet me at Ryan's. You know where Ryan's is at? I'll meet you there."

As the Burdens made their way out the side door of the church, one of Kennedy's parishioners—a deacon—passed them on the stairs.

"Was that . . . ?" the man said, doing a double take.

"Mm-hmm," Kennedy said to the deacon, fishing some more money out of his pocket. "Listen, go find the cheapest— somewhere decent, now—but go find the cheapest motel you can and set them up for a week."

"What? A whole *week*? You sure you wanna—"

"They been living in a truck with those kids, okay? They human beings. I don't care what you think about 'em, but we have to feed them.

"Besides," Kennedy said with a wink, "this New Beginning, ain't it?"

Everyone in the congregation knew well the story of the church's founding. Back in 1984, a young Reverend Kennedy had just resigned his post at a rural church in Abbeville County, and a fair portion of the congregation came with him. They met in schools, restaurants, living rooms, anywhere they could be together, and Kennedy spent weeks casting about for a name. One day he was ministering to one of his parishioners, an older gentleman, a wounded Vietnam veteran struggling with addiction issues. (Black and Hispanic soldiers, fighting a deeply unpopular war with no guarantee of their rights at home, were two to three times more likely to suffer from battle-related PTSD than white veterans.) "He told me, 'We did some things over there that nobody . . . I don't know if I can ever be forgiven.'" Kennedy talked with the man about his sacrifice and what it meant to find forgiveness through Christ. At last the veteran said, "If you telling me that God can give me a fresh start, a new beginning in life—then that oughta be the church name. I think the church should be called New Beginning."

And so it was.

Kennedy knew his decision to help one of the chief architects behind the Redneck Shop would raise eyebrows. The reverend was no miracle worker, and he didn't yet know how the situation would play out—whether his generosity might truly spark a change, or if Mike Burden would, in effect, take the money and run. But he didn't second-guess himself, either. "I was raised to love your enemies, and to pray for those who despitefully use you," he said later. "And lemme tell you something: God see ya. And his judgment is serious. All of this will come to play on Judgment Day. That's my belief. That's my faith."

RYAN'S, THE BUDGET steakhouse and buffet chain, had opened a location across from the church that April, to considerable fanfare, and quickly became Rev. Kennedy's favorite restaurant—

though Burden already knew that from the weeks he'd spent stalking the reverend. The whole congregation would meet there after protests and planning sessions. Kennedy himself stopped in as often as two or three times a week. Catfish, corn-bread, mac and cheese, five separate Mega Bar buffets, and a bakery, all you could eat for little more than six dollars.

"Can we bless this food right quick?" Kennedy said after the odd dinner party sat down with their plates.

Mike half bowed his head, one eye trained on the reverend.

Blessing completed, Kennedy lifted his fork. "So, tell me what happened."

Mike was slow to talk at first, but gradually he began to describe the argument he had had with John Howard, the seven years he had spent working for the man without a steady pay-check, the way he and his family had been unceremoniously tossed out on the street. And he talked about Judy, how she had been right about the Klan and about John. Given the chance to do it all over again, Mike said, he would make the same choice—to leave—but now he was right back where he'd started all those years ago. No job, no home. Every so often the reverend asked a question about Mike's goals, his plans for the future, what he hoped to accomplish—questions Mike was in no way prepared to answer that night. But to Mike and Judy's surprise, the rever-end didn't seem remotely interested in discussing the Redneck Shop or the inner workings of the Klan. "He just wanted to talk to us as *people*," Judy said. "He wanted to know what he could do to help, to get us lifted back up."

At that question, Mike pushed his food around the plate. "To be honest, I would like for me and my family to move away from this town."

"What's stopping you?"

"Money."

Kennedy could understand that. His thoughts drifted briefly to the multicultural center, where construction would soon stall for lack of funding.

"That shop," Mike continued, "it ain't caused nothing but problems. And I'm gonna find a way to pay you back for your kindness today. I'll paint the church, or . . . whatever needs done. I'm good with my hands."

Kennedy shook his head. "There's something else you can do for me."

Burden felt himself tense up involuntarily. Accepting a free meal for his stepchildren and working off that debt through manual labor was one thing. The suggestion of some larger commitment was another thing entirely. "It was like, how far do I trust?" he says.

But the issue of trust was Kennedy's point exactly. "I think you should speak to the congregation," Kennedy said. "Tell 'em what you told me, that you're done with the Klan. You go up there and show 'em who you are, and they'll . . . accept you more."

"He said it would be like a peace offering," Burden recalled. "Because at the time, I think his congregation—they felt a lot like me. They had trust issues, too."

After dinner, Mike and Judy climbed back in the truck and headed west. In the cab, Stacy and Brian were already half asleep. The light from the dashboard cast a glow on Mike's face.

"How does it feel?" Judy asked.

"What?"

"That the man you was gonna try to kill is helping us."

Mike was quiet for a long time. "I don't know," he said finally. "I can't figure out what's in it for him."

. . .

TWO NIGHTS LATER, Rev. Kennedy looked out at a sea of faces from the carpeted riser of his modest pulpit. "This is a very special night," he said. "Tonight, our little town becomes a town to be imitated. We're not saying our problems are over. Our fight continues. But we are proud of what's happened this week."

Burden's public apology, which had been billed in the local papers as a "unity service," had brought out a sizable crowd. Every pew was full, with church members and a number of city and county officials. All ten members of the choir were assembled to Kennedy's left, seated on two parallel rows of brown metal folding chairs. And in the front row, dressed in jeans and muddy sneakers, was Mike Burden, his knee bouncing uncontrollably.

He was perhaps right to be nervous. On the surface, the congregation at New Beginning was warm and welcoming, if a little tentative. Behind the scenes, however, there had been plenty of chatter: *You know he a Klansman. We oughta run him outta here.* Some members had worked up the courage to confront their pastor directly: Why in God's name would he help the very people who had caused the congregation so much pain? What exactly was he trying to prove, anyway?

"I told them I'm not taking up for the *Klan*," Kennedy said. "I'm taking up for God's creation. I don't care how evil they are—you have to be careful not to become like them. That's the difference between the Klan's ideology and the teachings of the Bible."

Whatever doubts his parishioners harbored about the young Klansman or the gamble their pastor was taking, Kennedy was not dissuaded. He figured his flock would come around. He realized, too, that at most his congregants had only read about the events of the previous few days, heard the story secondhand. Actually being there, and seeing the humiliation on Burden's face, was different.

Not long after the Burdens had climbed into their truck and driven to Kennedy's church, the Laurens police chief, Robin Morse, had attempted to broker a meeting between Mike and John so that the Burdens might retrieve their belongings without the need for a court order. Mike was informed that he could return to the shop on Tuesday morning and pick up his things with the safety of a police escort. Later that evening, however, as the Burdens were sitting down to dinner with the reverend, Howard reneged on the deal.

They had arrived at the Redneck Shop to find everything they owned piled in a heap at the back of the store—their clothes covered in mud and reeking of urine; cardboard boxes scattered over the lawn, the bottoms soaked with dew and disintegrating. Their larger possessions, they would later discover, had been trucked out to a storage facility in Woodruff, thirty minutes away. The rest was just gone. "I had a jewelry box," Judy said later, "and my mom and my grandma had given me certain little pieces. It wasn't really worth a lot, but . . . it got gone. Stolen. Stuff you cannot replace." Mike and Judy had to pick through their possessions under the watchful eye of the press, fielding questions from reporters who were anxious to know about the details of the argument, the future of the shop, and what exactly a black preacher was doing helping a Klansman.

"Need has no respect of race or ideology," Kennedy told the reporters gathered behind the shop. "One thing we do at New Beginning is we help anyone in need."

Back at the church, the reverend beckoned his new parishioner to the pulpit. Burden slid out of his seat and paced to the front. He looked at rows and rows of black faces, some smiling, some scowling, little kids yawning and swinging their feet, old men in their double-breasted blazers, and a large portion of the reverend's family lining the first pew. And he looked at Judy. She smiled and gave him a little nod.

"I want to apologize for opening the Redneck Shop," he began. He told the crowd about his reasons for joining the Klan, about why he'd chosen to leave, and the remorse he felt for the "heartache" the shop had caused. He admitted that a disagreement with John Howard had spurred his decision to relinquish the license, but vowed to do whatever he could to ensure that the shop stayed closed. He heaped praise on his wife, who he explained had been instrumental in helping him see the error of his ways, and thanked Reverend Kennedy, the only person who had been willing to step in and save his family from homelessness. Then, sensing that the congregation might be suspicious or unwilling to believe that he'd had a change of heart, he made a plea: "I risked my home. I've risked my family's reputation. I've risked my family's life. Now I'm asking you to trust me. Y'all have to trust me, because I have to trust you."

At the end of Burden's speech, Rev. Kennedy got up again to lead the congregation in prayer. The choir sang a few gospel songs, and the service came to a close. Some folks were still wary. Others were eager to speak to the Burdens one-on-one, to hear more about Mike's sudden conversion.

"See, I knew Judy," Clarence Simpson said. "I used to manage a rent-to-own—that's how I got to know Judy and Carl, doing business with them. Nice, sweet people. The children? Very nice. People you would really want to do business with . . . If the reverend showed love and mercy, so to speak, why shouldn't I?"

As the crowd milled about in the sanctuary, Kennedy pulled Mike aside and explained that one of his deacons had a few rental properties, and that one might be available. "Would you be interested?"

Burden shook the reverend's hand. "I'll take anything."

"Now, THIS PARTICULAR street here—this is a black community, right?"

Clarence is driving his Cadillac SUV roughly ten miles an hour through a modest neighborhood situated a little ways north of the courthouse square—incidentally, the neighborhood where he grew up. "But, see, white folks used to live here, too," he says. "This is Washington Street, but back then it was known as Stumptown."

There are, or at some point were, thousands of unofficial "stumptowns" spread across the country—many of them poor African American communities, most of them named for the tree stumps that remained after land was cleared for new development. Laurens's version was settled after the turn of the twentieth century, and grew further still after the Second World War, when the need for modern housing exploded. (By 1940, 70 percent of the homes in Laurens County still had no running water; three-quarters had no bathtub.) Like all neighborhoods in Laurens, Stumptown was segregated, but it had long been a place where many poorer residents—black and white—could find a place to call their own.

"Everybody owned their own home here at one time," Clarence is saying, "but they all died out. These are all just empty now." Floating past the car windows, in slow motion, are rickety bungalows and little one-room frame houses with weatherboard siding; the buildings sag and lean and sigh with age.

Switchgrass has grown up and over and through the cement steps of one home's porch, busting them apart. The plastic rain gutter on another has cracked and sheared off from the roofline. There are small signs of life—a pole-mounted satellite dish here, an overflowing recycling bin there—but Stumptown for the most part is eerily quiet. Clarence slows to a stop just shy of a rural intersection and lets the car idle.

"See that yellow pole there?" he says. On the far side of the intersection is a bright yellow sheath of plastic encasing a tension cable at the base of a telephone pole. Beyond it, Washington Street slopes downhill for a hundred yards or so before dead-ending at a gravel railway embankment. "That's where the white people lived, back down there. Black folks lived on this street, white people there. But you better believe the white people that stayed down there, they were poorer than us black folks. They *hated* us, too. They really hated us."

Off to the right is a plot of land, overgrown and unkempt, hemmed in by a chain-link fence. Somewhere beyond is the former home of one particularly cantankerous white neighbor. "He would come up in his car and try to run over the black kids that'd be in the yard. I mean, this is how bad the hatred was."

Clarence turns his car around and drives the other way down Washington, deeper into the black part of town. To the east lies a dense swath of pines. To the west, visible from the crest of the hill, are the golden arches of a McDonald's and, farther afield, the smokestacks of Laurens Cotton. At the bottom of the hill, Clarence pulls to a stop in front of the corner lot and gestures to a single-wide trailer, tucked into the hillside and propped up by a cinder-block foundation.

"This was *my* first home. This is where my wife and I lived when we got married in 1970."

The trailer has eggshell-colored steel siding and a corrugated metal awning balanced awkwardly atop wrought-iron columns. Four mismatched windows dot the façade, all different shapes and sizes.

By the time of Burden's falling-out with Howard, Clarence and his wife had long since moved "to the country," a simple ranch home amid the vast tracts of farmland west of Laurens— but they kept their first marital home as a rental property. By chance, a tenant had vacated just before Burden's apology to the church, which is how the former Klansman and his family came to reside in a black neighborhood. Stumptown would be their home for the next eleven months.

Moving in didn't take long, as most of the couple's possessions were still locked up in storage. It wasn't until then, however, that Reverend Kennedy realized just how much Burden had relied on the Klan, and specifically on John Howard. "He would buy Mike shoes," Kennedy said. "Buy him a shirt, buy him a pair of pants, but never give him money. I asked, why? Because if he had his own money, he wouldn't be dependent."

Mike had gone in search of work and even talked his way into a few handyman gigs—painting a house, tiling a bathroom— but it wasn't enough. Though he had renounced the Klan, the press coverage had associated his name, permanently, with the face of white supremacy. "Everybody that you used to go to see and talk to more or less ignored you," he said. "Door got shut in your face real fast. And then you got people out there that are supposedly in support of the church, in support of getting rid of the Redneck Shop. But when it came down to actually doin something, and makin it possible so I could get in and get a job, they done the same thing. 'Cause they didn't want no conflict."

There weren't many jobs to be had, anyway. Between December 1995 and July 1996, the unemployment rate in Laurens

County jumped to 7.6 percent. Roughly a thousand jobs had evaporated within the span of eight months.

Without John Howard's patronage or any kind of income, Mike and Judy came to rely on the reverend. "He would call us up and say, 'We just had a big donation of clothes. Come up here and see if anything fits.' Or 'Do y'all want to come to the church and eat with the Soup Kitchen?'" When the power bill arrived and the Burdens couldn't pay it, they resorted to candles and a camping stove—that is, until Rev. Kennedy had the utilities turned back on in his name. At one point, Burden was forced to sell his truck, and the family started relying on church members for transportation.

Going out in public became increasingly difficult. One day, Stacy came home from school crying because some of her classmates had called her a "nigger-lover." At Walmart, Judy and the kids were spat on by a grown woman who was upset they'd turned their backs on the Klan. "It got to where we didn't even want to go to no stores," Judy said, recalling that she felt most comfortable when Kennedy was with them. People were less likely to treat you poorly if a pastor was around. The day Mike relinquished the license to the Redneck Shop, Judy had told reporters that she had "never been prouder of a person than I am of my husband." She had not anticipated the isolation or the blowback she would receive from so many people in the community. As for Burden, he would later tell a reporter from *The State*, "I think I'm learning what hate feels like."

JOHN HOWARD WAS in a bind. The very steps he had taken to secure his business—chief among them applying for a license in his former protégé's name—were now the very things keeping him from it. Shortly before noon on Tuesday, the day after Kennedy took Burden in, Howard marched into City Hall and asked to speak with the city administrator, Gene Madden.

"I wasn't here," Madden later explained to the *Greenville News*, "but he requested a transfer of the business license." The city of Laurens, however, had an ordinance that prohibited the transfer of such a license from one party to the next. Instead, Howard was informed, he would have to reapply and go through the process all over again. Upon hearing this, Howard grew angry and swore to the clerk—to anyone who would listen, really—that they would all be hearing from him again, this time through his lawyer.

The scene kicked off a fevered round of speculation in the press: What would Howard do next? And when would he do it? Calls to the Howard residence either went unanswered or, more frequently, ended with the Redneck Shop's proprietor abruptly slamming down the telephone. Madden, meanwhile, made it clear that if Howard moved to reopen the shop, the license wouldn't be granted without input from the City Council. Behind the scenes, city officials had been weighing the grotesqueries of the shop against the demands of the First Amendment, a topic with which they were all now very familiar. After various Klan factions sued for, and won, their right to rally in towns across the Upstate, no one was taking the decision about the future of the Redneck Shop lightly. They also knew plenty about Suzanne Coe. The defamation suit against Councilman McDaniel had stalled briefly due to a clerical error, but the councilman, despite having claimed that he wouldn't "spend 15 cents" to defend the suit, had resorted to hiring a lawyer.

"They should be extremely careful," Coe warned reporters, speaking about the City Council. "[Howard] is going to apply for a new license. If they do not issue a new license, they had better have one extremely good reason that isn't just the fact this is the Redneck Shop."

The "extremely good reason" city officials were banking on was a potential loophole within the city ordinance, which stated that a license could be denied "when the application is incomplete, contains a misrepresentation, false or misleading statement, evasion or suppression of material fact, or when the activity for which a license is sought is unlawful or constitutes a public nuisance." The problem, of course, was that the ordinance didn't specify what "public nuisance" meant.

"A nuisance," Coe said, "would be something like a club that is so noisy, people can't sleep around it. . . . The Redneck Shop is objectionable to a whole lot of people, and that is completely valid. But just because it's objectionable doesn't mean you can ban it."

The days until the next City Council meeting ticked by, with nary a word from John Howard. Finally, on Tuesday, July 16, six of the council's seven members gathered in the council chambers, a small wood-paneled room on the second floor of City Hall. Shortly after the proceedings were called to order, Gene Madden rose to address the room. "We must balance the applicant's First Amendment rights against the council's duty to protect its citizens against private interests [that run] counter to the public good. I recommend that the request, when it comes, be denied."

The council retired for a thirty-minute executive session— a closed-door, off-the-record meeting—to receive input from Thomas Thompson, the city attorney. Upon their return, Marian Miller, the council's sole African American woman, made a motion to accept Madden's recommendation. Councilman

James Robertson seconded that motion. The remaining members quickly followed suit, launching what was in essence a preemptive strike.

The following day, the editors of the *Laurens County Advertiser* praised the council's decision: "We believe the city is on firm ground in denying the application. . . . [Closing the shop] was more than just the moral thing to do."

"This time," Madden said, "we feel like we stood for something."

NOBODY AT NEW Beginning expected the Burdens to become full-fledged members of the church. Kennedy had helped plenty of people in this way before, but his good deeds in the community rarely resulted in a larger crowd on Sunday mornings or more money in the collection plate. As the weeks slipped by, however, Judy's relationship to the church grew stronger. To her, Kennedy's arrival in the parking lot outside the police station that morning had been nothing less than divine intervention. "I mean, I always believed in God. My savior Jesus Christ," she said. "But as far as me going to church? No. Not before this. But I believe He sent Reverend Kennedy there to help me, I really do . . . And I really enjoyed going to Reverend Kennedy's church. I felt the spirit."

Mike, on the other hand, was quiet and skittish, which did not necessarily make him any easier to trust. "He was resisting *who* was helping him, so to speak," Clarence said. But one morning, something shifted.

"We usually arrived at the church first," Clarence says, "and they would come and sit with us. And one morning he told me, 'I love Judy, and she loves coming here, and I'm gonna get on board.'"

Clarence had been among those urging Burden to come more often to Sunday services.

"You don't think they mind?" Burden asked, gesturing to the folks filing into pews.

"*Mind?* No, they don't mind. We don't see no race in here."

The truth was that Burden was desperate for reassurance. "Mostly he wanted to be assured that the congregation had nothing against him," Clarence said. "He didn't want to leave a whole bunch of men who cared about him"—the Klan—"to come to a congregation that didn't care about him. He wanted the love and affection of the congregation to surround him."

Burden's need for reassurance was just as evident when he finally admitted to Kennedy how close he had come to taking the reverend's life. Judy had insisted on it, had been insisting on it for weeks, in fact, until she finally dragged Mike to the church and sat him down in the reverend's office. "She was real serious. You oughta see Judy when she get serious," Kennedy said. "And she said, 'If we're going to have any kind of future, he's gonna have to talk to you. Tell you everything.' "

Having thus deposited her husband, she gently closed the door behind her. "I'm going to leave you two alone now."

Both men stared at each other for a moment in silence. Mike got up and began pacing along the narrow space just beyond the reverend's desk. "I don't know how to tell you," Burden began.

"Just tell me."

"There's certain . . . *words* you won't like."

"Don't worry about the words. I don't care how you have to say it. Just give it to me plain."

Kennedy settled into his chair as Mike began to describe the conversations he'd had with John Howard, the weapons stockpiled inside the shop, how Howard had described the reverend as a thorn in his side. "John Howard wanted me to kill you," Mike said.

"And . . . ? Keep going?"

The casual nature of the question—the same tone Kennedy had used with the police officer, months before—brought Mike up short. This wasn't quite the reaction he had anticipated.

"Were you going to do it?" Kennedy asked.

Burden took a deep breath and then nodded. He described having climbed onto the roof on the night when Kennedy followed the angry young couple to the Redneck Shop, an evening when Kennedy had anticipated the potential for violence. To hear that a young Klansman had been dispatched as a kind of security measure was not particularly surprising. But then Burden began to describe a different evening, a time the reverend didn't remember.

"That night, you were right there on 221 at the convenience store," Burden said.

Kennedy sat up a little in his chair. "What night?"

"He told me the exact night," Kennedy remembered later. "I had left the Greenwood-Abbeville area, and I was on my way home." A little ways outside of town, the reverend stopped for gas at a convenience store beside the highway. Burden explained that he'd been following Kennedy for weeks, that he'd been waiting for an opportunity, a moment when the reverend was alone and vulnerable. On his way inside, however, Kennedy ran into the grandson of one of his older white friends, a boy he knew well and with whom he had a fond relationship. "He was like the leader in his group, and since he liked me, all these kids got around me." Kennedy had been flanked by the group of chatty white children on his way inside the store, and they followed him all the way back to his vehicle after he'd paid. He hadn't been alone at any point, which he now realized might have been the thing that saved him. "I remember that night, and I said, 'My God.'"

"I hate to tell you all that," Burden said when he had finished his confession. And then, with a sort of childlike innocence, he asked, "You mad at me?"

"I'm glad you felt the freedom to talk to me," Kennedy said. "But we just have to get you on your feet, help Judy take care of those kids."

If the reverend felt uncomfortable, or doubted the sincerity of his newest parishioner's conversation, he did his best not to show it. His family, however, felt differently about the strange man who had joined the congregation. They wondered if the whole thing might have been some sort of plot to gain greater access to the reverend. They became more watchful, a little more suspicious.

"There were many times we would go to the church with prayer in our heart," Pam, the reverend's sister, said. "Even opening his office door, wondering and not knowing . . . would we find him alive?"

eight

"LET'S TALK BUSINESS"

Three days after the Laurens City Council voted to deny him a new business license, John Howard sued the city in federal court. Officials may have thought they were stepping up to do the right thing—"standing for something," as city administrator Gene Madden described it. But it turned out that by refusing to accept Howard's application for processing, failing to provide a written reason for the denial of a license, and denying Howard the right to address City Council in executive session before the decision was made, the city had violated a number of its own bylaws. Laurens City Code Section 11-37c plainly stated that no person should be "subject to persecution for doing business without a license" unless he or she first had been granted the chance to appeal.

"The city has simply chosen to disregard all its own procedures," Suzanne Coe told the *Clinton Chronicle*. "They're doing this kind of like a kangaroo court."

The lawsuit, filed on behalf of Howard in U.S. District Court in Greenville on July 20, asked for damages, attorneys' fees, a reversal of the city's ruling, and a declaration that the Redneck Shop was not a "public nuisance." "I don't agree with many things Mr. Howard says," Coe explained, "but I don't believe the First Amendment should be compromised simply because you're offended."

In the meantime, she advised her client to reopen the Redneck Shop, which Howard did—gleefully. He passed out photocopies of Section 11-37c to members of the press, praised his attorney, and touted the merits of his case during an impromptu press conference on the courthouse square. "When your own city council don't even know their own laws," he said, "it looks pretty bad for them." Ten days after being put out of business, Howard's store was headed toward a grand reopening.

"I knew it was going to happen," Burden said later. "What I done was just threw a monkey wrench in his spoke. I was tryin to shut the store down and get it eliminated, but I didn't have enough juice to do it."

In the meantime, he and Judy continued to rely on Rev. Kennedy and New Beginning for even the most basic of needs. Mike spent more and more time helping out around the church. "There'd be times when Rev. Kennedy would come by and say, 'Hey, can you come to the church and fix this?' Or 'My car is acting a little weird, would you look at this?'" he explained. "So it was kind of a trade-off, more or less."

In addition to working as a sort of on-call handyman for New Beginning, Burden was also frequently asked to recount the story of his conversion. It turned out that loads of folks wanted to meet the man who left the Klan and joined a predominantly black church. At one point, an entire congregation from Pennsylvania made the trek to Laurens in a big Greyhound bus.

"That church was just packed," Judy said later. "It was plumb full. They came all the way down from Philadelphia to meet Mike and me."

Though Judy may have been enjoying, for the most part, her newfound celebrity status, Burden was considerably more wary. He had only just gotten used to the members of Kennedy's congregation, had only recently come to trust that the people of New Beginning had no plans for retaliation or retribution. "Now I've got people from Philadelphia," he said later. "I don't know these people. And I'm tryin to be cordial, but I'm also on guard as well. Because I'm waitin on anything. *Anything.* It can happen that quick."

After so many years as the Klan's enforcer, tasked with spotting any possible threat to himself and other high-level members, Burden felt strange putting himself at the mercy of strangers. It took the better part of the afternoon for him to relax enough to enjoy chatting with the churchgoers who lined up to shake his hand or ask him questions.

"There was an older lady—she didn't shake my hand, she actually hugged my neck," he said. "And then she grabbed my arm, and she looked at me. Then she rubbed her arm and rubbed her hand and she goes, 'See? It don't rub off. It's all just skin color. We're the same underneath.'"

As the weeks slipped by and Howard's lawsuit worked its way through the court system, city officials came to understand just how much trouble they were in. By late summer, Howard had officially reapplied for a license (and been denied), but officials were compelled to let him do what he essentially had already been doing: operating the business as usual, pending results of the appeal process. In November of that year, Howard and his attorney were finally granted a private meeting with the City Council. Afterward, legal advisers warned that the city faced certain defeat should his case actually make it to trial. Granting him a license and abandoning the fight, on the other hand, would save taxpayer dollars and prevent the city from having to pay damages.

Rev. Kennedy could sense which way the wind was blowing even before he showed up to a City Council meeting in November and watched council member Johnnie Bolt motion to approve Howard's license. Mayor Taylor, in his capacity as chairman of the council, put the motion forward for a vote. "All in favor, raise their right hand."

Six hands shot up in the air.

"All opposed?"

Councilwoman Marian Miller was the only nay.

Standing in the back of the room, leaning against the wood-paneled wall with his hands clasped in front of him, Kennedy's voice was barely audible: "That's a disgrace."

An Associated Press cameraman had traveled to Laurens to document the proceedings that evening. Mayor Taylor, perhaps sensing the possibility of an on-camera confrontation, quickly adjourned the meeting. Kennedy followed him outside, however, and accused him of betraying the best interests of his citizens. He then promptly got into a shouting match with Councilman Richard Griffin on the square. "I have no respect for a city that will approve the presence of a Ku Kluxer," Kennedy declared, vowing to continue his protests. But even then, he knew that city officials were finished with the fighting, and the Redneck Shop was likely back in business for good.

Later that week, the editors at the *Laurens County Advertiser*— who just four months earlier had praised council for denying the license—now praised the decision to grant one. "We would encourage residents not to patronize the shop. The battles up to now only have served to give the business a bounty of free publicity it never could have afforded on its own and drawn numerous curiosity seekers to enter its doors. We hope that in the future, lacking the free publicity . . . the store will prove not to be economically viable and be forced to close or go bankrupt."

For Kennedy, the request to ignore the shop was the most frustrating reaction of all. After all those months of protests, very few people in Laurens seemed to grasp what he had been trying to tell them: the store was little more than window dressing for whatever the Klan was doing behind the scenes. No matter what the reverend said, he couldn't quite get the larger community to take the shop—and what it meant to African Americans in Laurens—seriously.

"Morally, I think [Howard] is wrong," Councilman Griffin had told reporters after his verbal altercation with the reverend, "but legally, when we start taking apart the constitution of the United States, then we will be called ignorant. My point is, I know when to fold 'em. We need to move on."

Rev. Kennedy didn't want to "move on." If the city couldn't deny Howard a business license before the fact, he thought, perhaps a case might be made to deny his license for *cause*—for violating laws that were already on the books.

According to Burden, Howard had taken advantage of some kind of loophole or grandfather clause, wherein areas of the building that weren't relevant to the business didn't necessarily have to be up to code. "What the inspector saw, the *active* parts of the building," Burden says, "we had set those up correctly. But other parts of the building wasn't really up to par. I mean, you had exposed wires, open circuits. A massive leak over a 480-volt breaker box—if water hit it, it'd put out a spark. Stuff like that."

By December, Kennedy was back in City Council chambers, asking for a series of "full and public" investigations. Specifically, he wanted details about how the shop managed to pass its building code and fire inspections and how its occupancy permit had been obtained. "If the city is not serious," he told reporters, "we are determined to do our own investigation."

While he waited for an official response from the council, Kennedy also set about trying to pursue a criminal case. Beyond his family and a few members of the congregation, he hadn't yet told anyone about Burden's confession of what happened that night on the roof of the Redneck Shop. Now he wanted to press charges—against John Howard, the mastermind behind the alleged plot. He hired a civil rights lawyer, and together they approached the State Law Enforcement Division. Burden, likewise determined to see justice done, readily cooperated with the ensuing investigation. He provided SLED agents with a voluntary statement, wherein he explained that Howard had described Kennedy as a "thorn in his side" and wanted something done about the troublesome reverend. He also sat for a polygraph examination.

It didn't help matters. To the questions "Did John Howard ask you to cause the death of Reverend David Kennedy?" and "Did John Howard give you guns and ammunition with which to shoot Reverend Kennedy?" Burden answered in the affirmative. The results of the examination, however, indicated deception in those answers.

For plenty of people in Laurens, Burden's conversion had been far too swift to be believable. Law enforcement officials had more than once expressed concern to Rev. Kennedy, privately, that Burden's change of heart might have been no more than a play for greater access. Others posited that Burden was just an opportunist, a man willing to say anything to anyone who would provide for his family. Kennedy's own attorney was somewhat skeptical about Burden's true motivations. "I trust David's instincts for the guy to some degree," he said warily in interviews with the *Los Angeles Times*. Only the reverend—and the members of his church—refused to lose faith in the newest congregant at New Beginning. "I'm not saying I can't be fooled," Clarence said. "But, no, Mike wouldn't have done what he did with Reverend Kennedy if he didn't really care."

The lack of any concrete evidence, however, coupled with the questionable polygraph, effectively shut down the SLED investigation into John Howard. Meanwhile, nothing ever came of Kennedy's requests for an investigation into the shop by the City Council. At every turn, he was stymied. And just as he feared, the Klan only continued to grow bolder.

At the state level, the debate over the Confederate flag had surfaced once again after Governor Beasley floated a proposal to remove it from the Capitol dome. (It was a surprising about-face for a governor who had supported flying the flag since his election in 1995.) At the next Laurens County Council meeting, McDaniel urged members to take a stand on the issue at the local level. "I'm tired of hearing the words 'I don't want to get involved' or 'I'm too old,'" he said. Support, however, was lukewarm.

Soon afterward, John Howard's friend and longtime associate Charles Murphy announced that he was opening a recruiting office on the second floor (i.e., the theater balcony) of the Redneck Shop. The goal, Murphy said, was to grow the

Keystone Knights into a political force that could challenge any lawmaker who supported removing the flag. "If you're in the legislature and vote to remove the Confederate flag," Murphy told the *Greenville News*, "[you] can start unpacking [your] desks. You're not going to be in office anymore."

Only months earlier, Howard had denied that he was recruiting people to the Klan; now his store was *advertising* a recruiting office. It was just as Kennedy had predicted: the more the community turned a blind eye to the shop in the square, the bolder the Klan would become in displaying their message.

Soon enough, that message arrived at Kennedy's doorstep. On Easter Sunday, 1997, the reverend's mother, Frankie, arrived at the side door of the church early in the morning, expecting to cook breakfast for the congregation. She started up the steps, and then stopped dead in her tracks. Plastered to the door was a Redneck Shop bumper sticker—the logo of the shop printed over a Confederate flag along with the words WE'RE HERE TO STAY.

After the church fires in the area and everything that had gone on with the shop, Kennedy and his congregation interpreted the sticker as more than just a prank. "The sticker was put on the door that I enter every day, the one that is closest to my study," Kennedy later told the *Clinton Chronicle*. The Laurens County Sheriff's Office looked into the vandalism and quickly determined that the sticker had been placed on the door sometime between ten o'clock on Saturday night and eight-thirty the next morning, likely intending for the congregation to discover it on Easter Sunday. Two fingerprints were lifted from the sticker, but they were never identified. SLED agents, meanwhile, interviewed five juveniles who claimed to have seen an unknown white male plaster a similar sticker to a stop sign about a half mile west of the church before hopping in his car and driving off, but that investigation never went anywhere, either: two witnesses claimed the man's car was white, one said the car was black, and two couldn't remember the color of the car at all.

When word got out about the incident, Howard denied his involvement. "Anybody could have done something like that," he told reporters, stressing that he'd given out stacks of bumper stickers in the past. "Reverend Kennedy has used this to start more racial overtones in efforts to create media publicity for his cause."

Weeks earlier, Kennedy had scheduled a meeting at the church for the Monday after Easter. He'd been planning a walk to the statehouse, a demonstration that would keep his fight against the shop front and center in state lawmakers' minds. "We'll be standing against the Redneck Shop, racism, and the Confederate flag," he had told reporters. "We'll be marching for better conditions for working people. It is all connected. We want to see a better America. We want to see a coming together of all people."

After the sticker was discovered, however, Kennedy changed the meeting from a planning session into a unity rally. Members of the choir sang "Amazing Grace," and the executive director of the NAACP's state branch, Brenda Reddix-Smalls, spoke in defiance of the vandalism. "We're not afraid of the Redneck Shop," she said to the crowd of about sixty. "We are not afraid of the Klan."

Michael Burden was there, too, once again sharing his story of escaping from the Klan, urging members to protect and stand by their church. No amount of rallies and speeches, however, could change the fact that many parishioners were starting to feel afraid. Wilhelmina Bates, Kennedy's aunt and a member of the choir, said to the *Greenville News*: "Every time we hear a sound, you can't concentrate. When we open a door, is it going to blow up?"

The Easter celebration and the next day's rally marked a turning point at New Beginning. For the first time, Kennedy noticed that some members of his congregation had opted to stay home rather than come to services. He didn't know it then, but that day would mark the beginning of a steady, slow decline in the church's attendance.

MAYBE IT WAS the sticker that finally pushed him over the edge, or the fact that the Redneck Shop was still open for business even after it had cost him so much. But as winter turned into spring, Burden was desperate. Even with continued support from the church, he couldn't get on his feet financially, couldn't provide for his young family. His stepchildren were still being harassed at school, and Judy was consumed with worry over how she would feed and clothe them. "We were broke and we needed money to pay rent and power, to buy food and stuff," she said later. "I told Mike, 'There's only one way I can figure out how to do it at this point.'"

Burden had already sold his truck for spending money. He had only one real asset left to his name—even if he was only a partial owner. Selling that asset was perhaps his only chance to turn his life around, not to mention pay Kennedy and the church back for their kindness. So one day in mid-April, a few weeks after Easter, Burden and his wife arrived at New Beginning with a proposal for the reverend: they wanted him to buy their remainder interest in the Redneck Shop.

Kennedy was, suffice it to say, reluctant. He was uncomfortable with the implication that Burden owed him anything, or that his church had helped someone in need with the expectation of later collecting on the debt. "We were not helping you to put you in bondage to us," he said to Burden. "We helped because it was the right thing for us to do."

"I know that," Burden said. "But I want you to have it. You helped us out when nobody else would."

As Kennedy considered the offer, his mind flooded with thoughts. His plans for the multicultural center had never gotten off the ground because he could never raise enough money. But what if he could turn the Redneck Shop into a place meant to foster racial tolerance? In the meantime, if Kennedy owned the building, maybe he could require Howard to comply with his requests for inspections. Maybe he could get the City Council to take his concerns more seriously. What if this was the thing he'd been praying for—the chance to close down the shop for good?

"Okay," Kennedy said. "You want to talk business, let's talk business. How much you asking for it?"

Burden smiled. "One thousand dollars."

It took Kennedy several days to discuss the strange proposal with members of his church, to run the decision by his advisers, and to rake together the money, but on April 23, he and the Burdens visited a real estate attorney in Laurens to sign the necessary paperwork. Within days, the sale of the Redneck Shop to a predominantly black church sparked a fresh round of attention in the national press. The "redneck and the reverend," as they were called, sat for interviews with *ABC Nightly News* and a slew of national newspapers, and Kennedy started to revel in having struck an unlikely blow against the Klan and John

Howard. "I'm his landlord," he told the *Washington Post.* "I know he's about to go out of his mind."

THE PRIDE OF the Piedmont Jubilee is an annual county-wide carnival in Laurens, a three-day festival featuring food, arts and crafts, live entertainment, and a fireworks show, with booths and balloons and activities set up around the square and at the county fairgrounds down on East Main Street. That year's festivities were marred, however, by yet another incident at the Redneck Shop. Three black children, ages eleven and twelve, and a twenty-eight-year-old disabled man, also black, were standing outside the store when Dwayne Howard, John Howard's thirty-one-year-old son, leaned out the door and blasted them with pepper spray. When police showed up and arrested him, Dwayne told them that the kids had been "aggravating him."

Almost immediately after purchasing Burden's remainder interest in the Redneck Shop, Rev. Kennedy had set about trying to enforce his rights to the property, in part by investigating the condition of the building. "We would like for our attorney to lead us into an inspection," he had explained to the *Laurens County Advertiser.* What he perhaps did not understand at the time of purchase, however, is that he didn't really have many rights when it came to the store. Kennedy wasn't *really* Howard's landlord, a fact the disgruntled shop owner was quick to point out when questioned about the sale. "How can a person be your landlord if he doesn't get any rent from you?" Howard said. And while there was some question about Howard's official responsibilities—Kennedy had been advised that life estate owners were typically responsible for keeping their property in good repair—that was a legal issue to be determined by the courts. Kennedy and his lawyer decided not to pursue it further until after Dwayne's assault trial.

In the meantime, he had plenty of other issues to protest. When Kemet Corp., a local electronic parts manufacturer based in Simpsonville, announced plans to shift a thousand jobs from the Carolinas to Mexico, Kennedy was there, marching alongside twenty other members of the Carolina Alliance for Fair Employment, shouting a call-and-response chant into his megaphone while parading up and down the road outside headquarters: "Who's unfair to the workers?"

"Kemet!"

"Who's sending jobs to Mexico?"

"Kemet!"

Weeks later, when allegations surfaced that an elderly prisoner at the Johnson Detention Center in Laurens may have been abused by guards mere hours before his death from acute pneumonia, Kennedy was there, organizing a protest of the entire Sheriff's Department.

However, on the afternoon in October when sixty members of the Keystone Knights decided to rally on the courthouse square, Kennedy was nowhere to be found. This time, the loudest protester in the crowd was Ed McDaniel. He shouted responses to various racist remarks, offered to debate the Klansmen "on any subject," according to the *Clinton Chronicle*, and invited any of the Klansmen to shake his hand—an attempt to bridge the divide, perhaps.

WITH THE MONEY from the sale of the Redneck Shop, the Burdens moved to a trailer in the neighboring town of Clinton.

They had hoped it would be a fresh start, that they could get back some sense of anonymity, that they wouldn't be so readily associated with the Klan and the controversy back in Laurens. "But it followed us right over there," Judy said.

Jobs were no easier to come by in Clinton. Every time Burden managed to land something—at a junkyard, working as a roofer—his employer would figure out his backstory and fire him. He started to travel farther and farther outside of Laurens to find work. At some point, Burden and Judy were both hired at Dispoz-O, a disposable plastics manufacturer up near Greenville. "They make the plastic sporks that you use at KFC," Burden said. But even a thirty-mile commute wasn't far enough. Within days, their boss had discovered the strange history of his new employees. "We didn't get *fired*," Burden explained, "we got 'asked' to leave."

On top of the job struggles, Burden also seemed to be drifting away from Kennedy's church. In mid-June, a collection was taken up to help him and Judy cover basic expenses, but he was growing tired of relying completely on the congregation. He started attending services less and less. And then all of a sudden, he stopped showing up altogether.

Reverend Kennedy and his deacon, Clarence, had both noticed the change in Burden's behavior. For one, he had grown clingy, needy, much less willing to let his wife out of his sight. "Mike always wanted to hang around Judy," Kennedy said. "He couldn't bear to be apart from her. Sometimes he didn't want to go to work." The reverend had chalked up Burden's behavior to some kind of attachment disorder. Clarence was a bit more blunt: "Jealous man can't work." Even Judy noticed the change. "I don't know if he was scared he was gonna lose me or what," she said. "Maybe I give him the 'family that he never had' type thing, and he was scared he was gonna lose it if he turned his back or let his guard down. I don't know."

As their financial situation became increasingly dire, as things looked more and more bleak, Burden only clung to Judy harder—until, finally, he was holding on way too tight.

In THE WEE hours of the morning on June 29, 1998, a Spartanburg County sheriff's deputy was patrolling the small town of Woodruff, about twenty miles north of Laurens. He turned onto Highway 101, a two-lane back road that winds through tree-lined tunnels and acres of farmland before turning onto Main Street at the south edge of town. Just past 4:00 a.m., he noticed two men moving about inside a gas station convenience store at a time when the business was supposed to be closed. The deputy cut his lights, parked his car, and headed to the rear of the building, where he waited to arrest the burglars as they exited. When he heard the back door open, he shouted from the darkness. "Stop! Police!"

Both men bolted for the nearby trees, but the deputy radioed for a helicopter and a team of tracking dogs. Less than a mile from the store, Michael Burden was captured by the dog team. He was released on bond the next evening.

Burden had told Judy that he'd gotten a job doing construction out of town and that he would need to be gone for a few days. "But instead of him going to work construction he was out stealing," she said later. "Breaking into places. He was trying to keep me and my kids in a home."

In fact, a string of robberies in Laurens and Spartanburg and neighboring counties—all following a specific pattern—had put the authorities on alert months prior to Burden's initial arrest. Once he got caught in the act, law enforcement officials now had a prime suspect for more than a half dozen break-ins. "They would hit businesses like convenience stores, golf courses, and bar-type places, but their favorite was convenience stores," Chuck Milam, an investigator with the Laurens County Sheriff's Office, later told the *Greenville News*. "And they never rushed into it; they'd case the places for a couple of days."

Burden was arrested again in early August by the Laurens County Sheriff's Department, after they amassed enough evidence to charge him with four counts of burglary and three counts of grand larceny. Within weeks, additional charges were handed down by the Clinton police. His bail was set at $35,000.

"I think they've been doing this for a couple years," Milam said. "They just got careless."

Burden sat in jail until his October indictment by a grand jury. In all that time, though, he never reached out to the reverend—or to anyone else. "I was on my own," he said later. "I got into it. It was my problem, and I was gonna get out of it."

This was one situation, however, that he couldn't talk his way out of. In February 1999, as part of a negotiated sentence, Burden pleaded guilty. He was sentenced to fifteen years, with three years of that suspended, plus five years of probation. He was under no illusions that his marriage would survive—he was still shy of thirty years old; his wife was just thirty-five, with two children to care for. "That's something I told her in the beginning," he said. "Go on with life. I didn't expect her to stay, waitin." But Judy was devastated. All of the suffering, the fights, and the energy she had spent willing Michael Burden to leave the Klan behind and start a new life, and now it was over. "I put my arms around him and I gave him a kiss goodbye," she said. "And that was it."

nine

THE SUBSTANCE OF THINGS HOPED FOR, THE EVIDENCE OF THINGS NOT SEEN

FALL 2007

"I know you wanted to get a copy of that deed," she said.

Reverend Kennedy had arrived at the Laurens County Clerk of Court's office, a beige industrial-looking building on Hillcrest Drive, to file some paperwork on behalf of his church. New Beginning owned, or in some cases had inherited, a slew of properties in the greater Laurens area—several parcels of undeveloped land, an old nursing home, a few vacant houses. It wasn't unusual for the reverend to pop into the office as often as two or three times a month. On that particular afternoon, Kennedy had asked one of the assistants to pull a copy of his deed to the Echo theater for his files. The assistant, however, was visibly distressed.

"There's two or three deeds on top of your deed," she said, holding a small stack of papers in her hand.

Kennedy waved her off. "I'm sure it's nothing."

"But there's two deeds *on top* of it. You need to pay close attention to that."

Kennedy leaned forward and glanced at the papers she was

holding, two additional deeds to the Echo theater, filed in 2006 and 2007, nearly a decade after he'd purchased the remainder interest from Michael Burden. He furrowed his brow. He hadn't made any changes to his ownership status, hadn't sold or even thought about selling his interest in the property.

"Rev," the assistant whispered, "are you *sure* you the owner?"

MICHAEL BURDEN'S COMEUPPANCE—a twelve-year prison sentence—should have been cause for celebration among the Klansmen he'd betrayed. Instead, it passed with little notice. By the time Burden was being shipped off to the maximum-security Kirkland Correctional Institution for reception and evaluation, Klan chapters all across the state were busy with troubles of their own.

In July, four members of Barry Black's Keystone Knights had been arrested for threatening the life of a police officer at a small rally in Boswell, Pennsylvania. A month later, Black himself was arrested in Hillsville, Virginia, for burning a cross "with the intent to intimidate"—a violation of an obscure statute that nonetheless carried a five-year prison sentence. The case would spend years winding its way through the legal system (going all the way to the Supreme Court, where his conviction was ultimately vacated), but in the summer of 1998, Black's future—and the future of his Keystone Knights—was anything but certain.

The Keystone Klan's troubles paled in comparison, however, to those facing the Christian Knights. Two years after filing suit, the Southern Poverty Law Center was finally bringing its arson case on behalf of Macedonia Baptist church to trial. In his opening statement, Morris Dees pointed across the crowded courtroom at a stoic Horace King and described a man consumed by hate, a man who offered his followers "protection" from their crimes, only to cut them loose when they got caught. Gary Christopher Cox and Timothy Welch, the men charged with setting the fires, testified in exchange for slightly reduced sentences; both said they regretted having been driven to violence by the Klan. "We were told we would not go to jail," Welch said on the stand. "We were convinced we were untouchable."

It was a strong case on those merits alone—but the SPLC's star witness turned out to be none other than Horace King himself. Dees played a video for the jury, taken at a rally in Clarendon County just a few weeks before Macedonia burned to the ground, in which King ranted and raved and shook with fury. "I tell you one thing," he screeched into the microphone, "the county I live in and the neighborhood I live in, they ain't no bubble-headed niggers livin in it . . . If you got a nigger livin on side of you, it's your fault."

And another, filmed during a rally in Washington, D.C.: "If we had this garbage in South Carolina, we would burn the bastards out!"

Video after video played to the stunned courtroom, revealing the ferocity of King's rhetoric and the brutal truth of his intent. In the end, it was an easy victory for the SPLC. The jury deliberated for all of forty-five minutes before handing down the largest verdict against a hate group in U.S. history: $37.8 million in actual and punitive damages—$12 million more than even Macedonia's lawyers had requested. Horace King was deemed personally responsible for $15 million, an unimaginable sum for a retiree in poor health living on little more than disability and Klan dues. His farm and his seven acres were deeded over to Macedonia, and investigators for the SPLC made it plain that any other assets, including future assets, would be seized in order to satisfy the judgment.

Dees called it a "day of reckoning." The Christian Knights were officially out of business, and Klan-watchers hoped that fear of similar lawsuits might drive other groups farther underground. "It could very well make them much more cautious in terms of public appearances and statements," Bill Moore, a political science professor at the College of Charleston, told the Associated Press. In South Carolina, the Klan was declared effectively dead.

But they were wrong. Less than two years after the trial, a new faction—the Carolina Knights—sprang up in the Christian Knights' place, led by a former acolyte of King's, an eighty-year-old preacher named Charles Beasley. Charles Gladden, a fifty-one-year-old plumber and former rank-and-file member of the Keystone Knights, ascended to the position of Grand Dragon and announced plans to march in Wagener, Salley, and Charleston. In the fall of 2000, in the hamlet of Burnettown, near the Georgia border, he was joined by a longtime associate: John Howard. Despite having insisted to reporters for years that he was retired, Howard donned his robes, hoisted a Confederate flag, and crowed that there was "a place reserved in the fiery pits of hell" for those who refused to rub elbows with the Klan.

The scandal surrounding the Redneck Shop, like all scandals, had lost its potency with time, fading considerably from public view in the ten years following Rev. Kennedy's acquisition of the remainder interest. Every so often, a reporter would nose around town, snap some photos of the "World Famous KKK Museum," talk to locals about the Confederate flag or illegal immigration or the legacy of slavery, and write up an article about the state of contemporary race relations. ("Slavery was eons ago," a Laurens bar patron once explained to a *Vice* reporter. "We're past that.") But for the most part, people just wanted to move on. Even the new mayor expressed a kind of resignation whenever she was asked to comment about the shop. "They're in business just like anyone else." The sigh was practically audible.

Actual goings-on at the Echo hadn't generated much news since the spring of 1997. The mural painted on the back wall— the Klansman on horseback—was replaced with a more palatable tableau: a portrait of Jesus, arms outstretched, hovering above a single eyeball and three interlocking rings, symbols associated with the Independent Order of Odd Fellows, a centuries-old (non-racist) fraternal order in which John Howard claimed membership.

Most residents had no idea the Redneck Shop had only grown more prominent among white supremacists, or that Howard was playing host to a far larger audience than a ragtag group of backwoods Klansmen. Beginning in 2002 or 2003, a Michigan-based neo-Nazi group chose the shop as the venue for its annual White Unity Christmas Party. At a 2006 gathering of the Aryan Nations—dubbed the Twenty-Fifth World Congress—more than 150 white supremacists of all stripes packed the meeting hall to hear speeches about the evils of blacks ("soulless mud people") and the depravity of Jews ("Satan is their father"), interspersed with information about the benefits of "leaderless resistance."

Virgil Griffin was there, telling those in the audience to "get every weapon you can get."

He was followed onstage by a South Carolina–based Aryan Nations officer, sporting on his biceps the double lightning-bolt insignia of the Schutzstaffel. "You want to see blood in the streets?" he hollered. "I do!"

Afterward, attendees milled around the crowded lobby, where they could peruse the usual assortment of racist bumper stickers and T-shirts, as well as merchandise brought in specially for the event: *Workbench AR-15 Project*, for example, a how-to manual for assembling one's own assault rifle and flouting federal gun laws.

The 2006 gathering was the rare occasion when a journalist, John F. Sugg of the now-defunct paper *Creative Loafing*, was allowed to document the proceedings. Through the windows of the lobby, mere moments after the conclusion of the day's speeches, Sugg noticed a small black child, perhaps eight years old, ride past the Echo on a bright orange bicycle. John Howard, who had been sitting on a wooden stool behind the sales counter, sidled over to the front of the shop and waved his finger in the direction of the boy. "There's a nigger I'd like to hang."

The Klan wasn't dead—in fact, it was growing. Between 2000 and 2007, the Southern Poverty Law Center observed a 50 percent spike in the number of hate groups operating in the United States, as well as increased cooperation among groups on the far right, a trend largely attributable to a rising tide of anti-immigrant sentiment. "If any one single issue or trend can be credited with re-energizing the Klan, it is the debate over immigration in America," Deborah Lauter, civil rights director of the Anti-Defamation League, warned in a press release. The Klan was returning to its nativist roots. And just a few months after the Aryan Nations convention, the Redneck Shop would find itself in the news once again—this time for its association with a man named John Taylor Bowles, a neo-Nazi running for president of the United States.

Bowles, the party hopeful for the National Socialist Movement (NSM) in 2008, was a short man with a ruddy complexion and a youthful chubbiness about him. A Maryland native and thirty-year veteran of the neo-Nazi movement, Bowles had moved to Laurens earlier that year, making his campaign head-quarters at the only place in the country audacious enough to host such an effort. For his running mate, he needed someone with bona fides, someone who could give his campaign legiti-macy within the broader white supremacist crowd. He chose Wild Bill Hoff, who by then had left the Klan for the NSM and risen to the rank of "major," in charge of East Coast operations.

Bowles's presidential platform was absurdly ambitious. Upon his election, he promised free healthcare, free college education, low crime, low gas prices, zero-interest mortgages, a retirement age of fifty-five, and a 5 percent flat tax. His appeal to neo-Nazis lay in how he intended to pay for such promises: by no longer "wasting white taxpayer dollars on third world countries, no-win wars, and foreign aid to Israel." He also advocated sending nonwhites "back to their respective homelands."

"This," he said to a curious reporter from the *Columbia City Weekly*, pointing to the swastika on his armband, "is coming back into style again." He admitted that there were many differ-ent symbols his party could use, but that the swastika seemed "to do the trick."

"Trick" is the right word for it.

The National Socialist Movement had been an obscure, little-known group on the far-right fringe since its found-ing in the mid-1970s, long overshadowed by more prominent neo-Nazi organizations such as the National Alliance and the Aryan Nations. Things started to change in 1993, however, when the group's founder showed up at a Minnesota state leg-islative committee meeting in full Nazi regalia, a stunt that landed him on the front page of the *Minneapolis Star Tribune*. A year later, twenty-one-year-old Jeff Shoep assumed control of the party and immediately began agitating for attention. It worked. By the mid-2000s, the NSM had become the largest—and flashiest—neo-Nazi group in the country. Members dressed in Nazi-style brown shirts (or *Braunhemden*), jackboots laced tight to the knee, and red armbands bearing the swastika. Every event they organized was designed to attract maximum unrest. The bigger the spectacle, the more intense the media coverage. The more intense the media coverage, the more prospective members sought the group out. A 2005 rally in a crime-ridden, gang-infested neighborhood outside Toledo, for example, drew as many as six hundred counterprotesters and quickly descended into a four-hour riot, which generated international press attention. Within months, the NSM, which before the rally had had fifty-nine chapters in thirty-two states, grew to eighty-one chapters in thirty-six states.

Bowles's presidential campaign was just one more in a long line of publicity stunts. No one in his right mind—not even among the white supremacist crowd—thought Bowles would actually win the election. (According to campaign finance reports filed with the Federal Election Commission, Bowles raised a little more than $3,500 between the fall of 2006 and the summer of 2008.) The point of the White House run was to further increase the NSM's visibility and to bolster its membership ranks. The group's largest event in 2007—at which Bowles announced his candidacy—was an anti-immigration rally at the statehouse in Columbia, South Carolina, followed by a three-day national meeting in Laurens, hosted by the Redneck Shop.

To anyone with even a cursory knowledge of John Howard's forty-year career in the Klan, it would've seemed odd that he was suddenly palling around with neo-Nazis. This was a man who had preached about the legacy of William Joseph Simmons and the Klan's supposed roots in American patriotism. Back in 1996, the Keystone Knights had actually banned anyone wearing neo-Nazi uniforms, emblems, armbands, or insignia from its public and private functions. Yet Howard seemingly had no qualms about his new friends, nor did he mind when the Nazis wanted to paint over the back wall in the shop yet again: the Odd Fellows mural was replaced with side-by-side portraits of George Lincoln Rockwell (founder of the American Nazi Party) and Hitler, their faces superimposed over the American and the Nazi flags, respectively.

Howard's longtime friendship with William Hoff might have had something to do with it. More likely, however, is that he was looking to cash out. There were rumors in the larger white supremacy community that Howard, who was aging and in ill health, was looking to sell the Redneck Shop. (Despite the initial publicity surrounding Kennedy's purchase of the remainder interest, no one in Howard's circle seemed to realize that the shop was no longer his to sell.) When no one in the Klan ponied up, Howard turned to Nicholas Chappell, the treasurer for Bowles's campaign, an eighteen-year-old who had just inherited a large sum of money after the death of his stepfather. In a package deal, Howard sold both the shop and the Lanford property to Chappell for a total of $25,000. Once again, however, Howard reserved for himself a life estate—the right to live in his home and run his shop for the rest of his life. He had found himself a new Mike Burden.

REV. KENNEDY WAS stunned.

Sure enough, there were two deeds "on top" of his deed, staking claim to the Echo theater. The most recent, dated March 30,

2007, transferred ownership from Hazel Howard—John Howard's wife—to Nicholas Chappell, reserving a life estate for John. It was basically the same deal as Kennedy's 1997 transaction, only with his name swapped out for someone else's, as if Michael Burden had never sold him the building all those years ago.

Kennedy flipped to the next page. The second deed—the older of the two, dated November 16, 2006—was even more troubling. This deed purported to transfer Mike Burden's remainder interest to Hazel Howard. As he read through the paperwork, the story became clear: through a circuitous series of swaps, Burden and Howard had conspired to circumvent Kennedy's rightful claim to the property. They had transferred ownership to Hazel; Hazel then transferred ownership back to John. And there was no doubt about Burden's complicity: his signature was right there in black and white, notarized and witnessed by two parties.

Kennedy had heard rumors over the years that Burden had rekindled his friendship with John Howard, even though he was still incarcerated. The more pressing question was how two fraudulent deeds could have been filed in the first place. Kennedy tracked down a legal assistant named Donna Jackson—the same legal assistant who had prepared the fraudulent deeds for John Howard—who informed Kennedy that no one in her office had performed a title search to verify Howard's right to sell the Echo in the first place. Apparently no one in the clerk's office had vetted the deeds for legitimacy before recording them, either. Any number of steps might have prevented the error, but it seemed as though Howard had just gotten lucky. As for the incompetence, Kennedy was nonplussed. "That's South Carolina for you."

The discovery of those fraudulent deeds would mark the

beginning of a years-long journey to understand what had happened, and to reassert his claim to the Echo. Kennedy hired a lawyer, but in the meantime he decided to pay a visit to an old friend.

Kennedy phoned the prison chaplain at Northside Correctional Institution—a minimum-security facility in Spartanburg County—and set up an appointment to see Michael Burden. But as he waited in the visitation room, a drab room lined with large windows, through which he could see prisoners shuffling single-file toward visits with their friends and family, he wasn't quite sure what to expect—whether his former congregant would even agree to see him, let alone admit to the fraudulent deed transfer. And then, through the glass, he caught his first sight of Michael Burden in nearly ten years.

"I'm trying not to get tearful," Kennedy said later, "but when I saw Mike coming . . . his hair had turned gray. It was like watching a movie—everything had gone by so fast." Burden was then a few years shy of forty years old, still thin and lanky, but the boyishness had gone out of him. Tiny lines formed at the corners of his eyes. "I had to keep from breaking down," Kennedy said, "because if he had stayed with us he never would've gone to prison."

As Burden walked across the room, the reverend stretched his arms wide. "And he fell in my arms," Kennedy said, "just hugging and squeezing." They sat and chatted for a while as old friends, catching up about New Beginning and the members of Kennedy's congregation. Clarence had since left and become a reverend in his own church, Wateree Baptist. Judy and her children, now grown, were living and working in the area; Kennedy sometimes took up a collection for her when money got tight. Finally, Kennedy brought up the subject of the deed transfer. "I said, 'Mike, I have a paper from the courthouse, and there are rumors that you got back with John Howard. Did you join with him at any time to try and resell the Redneck Shop property?'"

Mike shook his head.

"I knew he was lying," Kennedy said later, "because his name was on the paper." And yet, as frustrated as he was by the deception, Kennedy still felt a measure of empathy for the man. Burden's collusion, Kennedy understood, was at that point less about ideology than it was an act of total desperation. Without Judy and the constant support of the church, Burden was in many ways more vulnerable than he'd been on the outside. "It makes me think about all the children caught up with the Klan and other hate groups," Kennedy said. "They just want to belong somewhere. They just want to feel a part of something, and unfortunately the wrong people nourish them and make them feel like they are important. So I always had to keep an opening for Mike. I didn't beat him up—'Oh, you lying.'"

Since Burden wouldn't admit his part in the deed transfer, Kennedy had little choice but to take his case to court. In the meantime, he could only hope that Burden might change his mind and once again gather the strength to defy John Howard. "When people get to the root of it," he later told the *New York Times*, "this is a horror story about what happens to young guys who are drifting and fall prey to the Klan."

By THE TIME Rev. Kennedy filed suit against John Howard, Michael Burden, and Nicholas Chappell in order to resolve the cloud on his title to the Echo theater, tragedy had struck the NSM. One day after announcing Bowles's and his campaign for the White House, William Hoff was killed in a car accident on

a rural stretch of Highway 146, not far from the Lanford property. Though he had five brothers and sisters, the only survivors
mentioned in his obituary were "two special and close friends,"
John and Hazel Howard, and an "adopted grandson," Dwayne.
Not long after his death, Hoff's brother Sheldon publicly revealed their family's biracial heritage, which he'd discovered
some fifteen years earlier when he got interested in genealogi-
cal research. (In the 1910 census, his father's family is listed as
black.) Sheldon had learned about Hoff's death while surfing the
Internet. "We don't have his ashes," he later told a reporter from
GoUpstate.com. "We don't even have a button from his clothes.
[The neo-Nazis] stole him in life, and they're stealing him in
death."

Bowles tried to make political hay out of the situation by
insinuating to reporters that Hoff's death was suspicious, but
the grandstanding eventually cost him. After publicly accusing the leader of the NSM of mismanaging funds and failing
to support his presidential campaign, Bowles was booted from
the organization. He promptly formed his own splinter group,
the National Socialist Order of America, which failed to attract
many members and later disbanded after Bowles suffered a
massive heart attack. (Upon his recovery, Bowles joined up with
the American Nazi Party.)

As for the young Chappell, he refused to acknowledge Kennedy's claim to the Redneck Shop, telling a reporter from the
Canadian *National Post*, "Blacks think that they own everything. That's part of their nature, part of their mindset. I could
claim I own any building I want but that doesn't mean it's true."
Not long after the collapse of the National Socialist Order of
America, however, Chappell packed up and left Laurens. Once
again, day-to-day operations at the shop fell to John Howard.

And for the next three years, as Kennedy's civil case wound its way through the court system, Howard continued to sell his wares and "educate" people about the history of the Klan, cheerfully leading customers through the shop and pointing out photos and placards and bits of memorabilia like some kind of macabre museum docent.

Sometimes videos of Howard's proselytizing made their way to YouTube. In a clip posted to the site on August 24, 2010, Howard points to a framed snapshot of a man in a black cowboy hat, standing in front of a green pickup truck, holding a sign printed with the words PRAISE GOD FOR AIDS. "He's the one that killed those niggers down there in Birmingham, Alabama," Howard says. "All those kids at that church? He's the one that blew 'em up." Slick as a used-car salesman, Howard suddenly switches gears and starts to hawk his merchandise. "These stickers are not but two dollars each . . . You can get ya a Nazi sword—whaddaya call them damn things? Bayonets? Daggers? Fifteen dollars."

As the years ticked by, however, Howard's health began to decline further. By the time Kennedy's civil case finally made its way to court in the fall of 2011, the Redneck Shop was open for business only one day a week.

Howard's defense at the non-jury trial was to plead ignorance. In sworn depositions, he admitted that he had heard Kennedy claim to own the theater, but that he'd brushed off the claim as implausible, if not ridiculous. "I figured it was Reverend Kennedy just raving up and down the streets: *I'm gonna close him.* And I ignored it . . . I figured the man was crazy."

Michael Burden, meanwhile, denied having any knowledge or memory of signing over the deed to New Beginning, and claimed that he'd been struggling with addiction issues back in the 1990s. "I was drinking and doing drugs at the time," he said in his deposition. "My memory back then was fogged with drugs and alcohol and I had my own problems. . . . My memory's vague—very vague back then because of what I was doing and the problems I was having myself."

"Nonsense," Judy said later when she heard about Burden's testimony. "Mike drank like two or three beers and he would be puking. He's not a big drinker. Never has been. And on drugs?"

"You couldn't get that man to take a Tylenol," Stacy said.

Circuit Court Judge Frank R. Addy Jr. wasn't buying it, either. In his December 9 ruling, he wrote that "the evidence demonstrates that Mr. Burden was lucid, mentally sound, and not under the influence of any intoxicant at the time of the conveyance [to New Beginning]. . . . Despite contentions that Mr. Burden was impaired because of years of substance abuse, the record indicates that [he] was of sound mind and understood the legal ramifications of his actions. . . . I also find credible the testimony that, at the time of the conveyance, Mr. Burden had developed a spiritual relationship with [Rev. Kennedy], which also contributed to Mr. Burden's motivation for the transfer." The judge ruled both the 2006 and 2007 deeds invalid, confirmed Rev. Kennedy's ownership of the remainder interest, and ordered Howard and Burden to pay Kennedy's legal fees.

In the wake of the trial, John Taylor Bowles attempted to downplay the significance of the ruling. In remarks posted to a variety of white supremacist websites, he explained that Howard's original life estate was still valid. "As long as the Redneck Shop is alive and [Howard] can operate his business in the building, the American Nazi Party can hold its activities there as well. The sky did not fall and the ground did not open up." In reality, however, the trial severely damaged his reputation within the movement. The message boards at White Reference.com, a now-defunct white supremacist website, lit up with posts about how Howard and Bowles had duped the young Nick Chappell. "In this matter Nick Chappell is the one who really got screwed over," one user wrote. "Bowles [and Howard] should learn to be men for once in their lives and actually give that young man back his money, or at least attempt to start paying him back like a real Aryan would do."

There's no evidence, however, that Chappell ever got his money back. In emails purportedly written by Chappell and posted to WhiteReference.com, he claimed that he spent virtually all of his $263,000 inheritance on Bowles's presidential campaign, the Redneck Shop, and donations to other organizations within the movement. "My youthful ignorance proved to be a great weakness of mine," he lamented. "I don't associate with Bowles or any other organization at the moment."*

John Howard, meanwhile, had been dealing with an array of personal issues. Even before the completion of the trial, he and his wife, Hazel, divorced. Soon after, he reportedly suffered a stroke. Within months of the ruling, in May 2012, he vacated the property. After sixteen years, the Redneck Shop finally closed its doors for good.

LATER THAT FALL, roughly ten months after winning his lawsuit, Kennedy received a late-night phone call from the Laurens County Fire Department. He jumped in his car and sped off

---

* Chappell's retirement from the white supremacist movement was ultimately short-lived. By 2017, he was living in South Dakota with his wife and four children and had become a "reverend" in the Creativity Movement, formerly known as the Church of the Creator, a neo-Nazi group. As he explained to journalist Chris Hagen, he was busy preparing for RaHoWa—or racial holy war. "I do believe that eventually this will boil down to a race war as we have already seen with the riots in cities like Ferguson, Missouri, and Baltimore."

down the Highway 127 bypass, a thick plume of black smoke already visible above the trees. By the time he arrived on the scene, New Beginning had burned nearly to the ground. The official cause of the fire was ruled to be an electrical issue, though Kennedy was understandably suspicious. He will always wonder if the fire was actually an act of retaliation by the neo-Nazis who had gathered at the Redneck Shop, or some disgruntled members of the Klan.

Given all that had happened, given the loss of his church, the dwindling size of his congregation, the protracted fight for ownership of the shop, and the fact that he is often still ostracized in Laurens, it would be easy to think that his extraordinary kindness in taking in Michael Burden was somehow not worth it.

Burden's collusion with John Howard, however, was short-lived. After getting out of prison, he found a job at the Anderson plant in Clinton, manufacturing hardwood floors. Before long, he started working toward getting his trucking license, the job he'd always wanted and never before been able—or ready—to pursue. For the first time in his life, Burden gained a modicum of financial stability, a way to support and provide for himself. The trucking job enabled him to finally leave Laurens, and John Howard, for good.

"I can't never change the fact that I did what I did," Burden said later. "That'll be there forever. I do feel remorse. I do feel pity and shame for it. But everything's a lesson in life. If I hadn't been through that, I wouldn't be the person I am now. I do not support the Klan, and I do have remorse for some of the stupidity I was encompassed in. It took me a long time to find that inner peace, for the turmoil and the hatred and everything to dissipate. But it has."

In time, he was able to reconnect with Judy, but as friends.

"We've talked once or twice," she said, "and I wished him all the luck in the world. That's how I found out that he was a truck driver now, and I said, 'Well, good.' 'Cause he really wanted to do that back when we were together. He really wanted to do that."

Judy believes that Burden's brief collusion with John Howard was largely based on fear.

"He really done a number on Mike, he really did. I'm so thankful that he was able to get out of here."

As for her relationship with the reverend, she believes it's not an exaggeration to say that he saved her life. "I don't know what me and my kids woulda done back then if it hadn't been for Reverend Kennedy."

For several weeks after the church fire, Rev. Kennedy operated out of his vehicle. He and his wife delivered food to needy families, as the Soup Kitchen was temporarily closed. They hosted Sunday services at their home, packing the den with thirty or forty people each week. But it wasn't long before he got a call from a local businessman, Harry Agnew, who wanted to help the church get back on its feet. "New Beginnings does so much good in the community, and Rev. Kennedy has reached out to so many people," Agnew later told reporters. "I was honored to help." Agnew and Kennedy spent several weeks visiting properties around the county until finally settling on an industrial building on a quiet stretch of Route 76, between Clinton and Laurens, which Kennedy purchased with insurance money and private donations. In lieu of pews, the sanctuary was filled with rows and rows of chairs—donations from Ryan's, the same steakhouse where Kennedy and Burden had shared their first meal some twenty years earlier, gifted to New Beginning when the restaurant went out of business. The Soup Kitchen is housed in an adjacent property, and on most days there are more visitors to the pantry than to the church. Yet Kennedy is thankful. "It was a tremendous blessing," he said of the new building. "All that came together to allow it to happen was an incredible blessing from God."

The reverend is in his sixties now. He still protests all manner of injustice in Laurens, still rankles people with his fiery rebukes, still challenges people to reckon with the past—and remains a deeply controversial figure in Laurens. Yet he is surprised when people express awe or disbelief at his church's willingness to take in the Burdens.

"I never saw anything great in what we did," he admits. "Nothing phenomenal. It's what we do. If you can't be moved to see about the human condition, then something is wrong with you." He quotes the theologian Howard Thurman, author of the classic religious treatise *Jesus and the Disinherited*. "He wrote about fear, hatred, and hypocrisy—the three hounds of hell. They will track you and destroy you. They kill the spirit." Thurman, an African American writer and educator, is most famous for providing a religious framework for the leaders of the civil rights movement. His philosophy of nonviolence profoundly influenced Martin Luther King Jr. By invoking him, Kennedy continues in a long tradition within the black church of confronting injustice without succumbing to hatred.

He preaches less often than he used to, choosing instead to guide and train the next generation of ministers. When he does ascend to the pulpit, however, he speaks with the same passion and fire he had in the spring of 1996, demanding from his parishioners a commitment to fighting intolerance. At a recent service, he challenged his tiny congregation to examine their own good works.

"I wanna know," Kennedy thundered, "is your work speakin for ya? Have you fed the hungry, clothed the nekkid? Have you visited the sick? Have you visited those who are incarcerated? Have you taken in strangers that you did not know? Have you given water to those that are thirsty? Remember what Jesus said: whatever you did not do for the least of these, my brethren, you did not do for me."

Afterward, members of the small congregation milled around the sanctuary, discussing the upcoming youth retreat and making plans for Sunday supper. Reverend George Dendy, one of Kennedy's associate pastors and a recent addition to the New Beginning family, was eager to share a few anecdotes—from his childhood in the days just after integration, to the casual racism he still experiences every day, to the fights his pastor continues to wage in the name of injustice. "If anyone has a right to hate, it's Reverend Kennedy," he says. "But he doesn't, because the love of God has come in, and I am glad about it." He wants people to know about the sacrifices Kennedy has made in order to help so many others. It's why he joined the church in the first place.

"I came because I like what they do in the community," he says. "I wanna serve, so the soup line, the dinners? I just like being a part of that. And I'm amazed at the church not having but a few members, but yet feeding fifteen hundred people. I'm amazed that they got a food bank. So that let me know that God is doing some great things here, even if there's not great numbers." That's what keeps Kennedy's church going, despite everything that happened in Laurens, and despite all of the work that remains to be done. Dendy points to a verse from Hebrews 11: "Faith is the substance of things hoped for, the evidence of things not seen."

He believes good things are in store for the church, and especially for Rev. Kennedy.

"He's overdue for a blessing," he says.

AFTERWORD

Twenty years after the Redneck Shop opened its doors, Andrew Heckler's film about the events in Laurens finally went into production. *Burden* was shot on location in Jackson, Georgia, a rural community forty miles southeast of Atlanta, over five weeks in October and November 2016. A stand-in for the Redneck Shop was erected in an abandoned storefront just east of Jackson's courthouse square. The building was then outfitted with a replica of the Echo's metal marquee, and filled with T-shirts and bumper stickers and racist trinkets—near carbon copies of the merchandise John Howard hawked for more than a decade. In advance of filming, the county issued a press release to alert residents to parking and street closures in the area, and to offer the following warning: "The set dressing . . . will include placement of some Confederate flags in various scenes. We are asking that [people] take no offense and understand that while this is based on a true story, it is only a movie and is in no way a reflection of the spirit of our community today."

County officials needn't have worried. One night, not long after the marquee was nailed into place, Heckler received an urgent call from his production designer, Stephanie Hass. "You need to come down here," she said. "There are people inside to get into the store. They think it's real. They're ... *shopping.*"

Indeed, for the next several weeks, producers and production assistants fielded questions from yet more locals who were anything but offended.

When do you guys open?
This store is just what we needed!
This is the greatest thing to come to Jackson in a long time.

The fall of 2016 turned out to be an especially fraught time to film a movie about combatting racial prejudice. Upticks in hate crimes had been widely reported, as had eruptions of violence at rallies across the nation. Presidential elections aren't exactly notable for their civility; mudslinging and smear tactics are as old as politics themselves. But as scores of journalists and historians pointed out, much of the increasingly inflammatory and divisive language utilized on the campaign trail—the depiction of a nation in peril, besieged by immigrants, the "America First" sloganeering—bore an eerie resemblance to 1920s-era Klan rhetoric.

Something was brewing, and it was palpable on set.

Dexter Darden, a young African American actor cast in the role of Reverend Kennedy's son, has since spoken publicly about the night a car full of white men slowed to a stop as he was preparing to film a scene. One of the men hopped out, waved a Confederate flag in Darden's face, and said: "You don't fucking belong here. Go home."

"That's when I realized it was real," Darden later told audiences at the Sundance Film Festival. "Because of the election, people became bold and outright and outspoken. We were trying to make a movie about peace and love, and all we were receiving was hate."

The violence and volatility did not abate after Americans went to the polls. According to a report compiled by the Southern Poverty Law Center, nearly 900 "hate incidents" took place across the United States in the ten days immediately following the election. The months to come would bring the announcement of a ban on travelers from seven majority-Muslim countries, the assertion that a federal judge could not fairly preside over a case owing to his Mexican heritage, the declaration that a private citizen with the temerity to protest police brutality was merely a "son of a bitch," and myriad claims that the country was being "stolen" and overrun by "animals" (i.e., immigrants). Yet the sight of neo-Nazis and Klansmen marching through the streets of Charlottesville in the summer of 2017 still seemed to catch the nation by surprise. The overwhelming response to the spectacle of young white men chanting "You will not replace us" and assembling beneath Nazi and Confederate flags was one of disbelief. *How can this really be happening?* Within hours, the hashtag #ThisIsNotUs began trending on Twitter.

Racially motivated violence, however, has plagued every generation since the country's founding; meanwhile, race has successfully been made into a wedge issue in every presidential election. What happened in Charlottesville is not new, and it recalls the question Reverend Kennedy asked reporters when they first descended on Laurens two decades ago: "America would love to put all the blame on the Ku Klux Klan. But what allows this atmosphere that allows the Klan to become bold?"

• • •

JOHN HOWARD DIED in September 2017 after a long illness. In accordance with his wishes, there was no memorial service. His obituary mentioned nothing about his decades-long association with the Klan and described him as the "last surviving member of his immediate family." (Despite his three children, ten grandchildren, and ten great-grandchildren.) The tenor of the obit seemed to signal the end of something. Debbie Campbell, owner of the newly renovated Capitol Theatre and Café, recently explained to the Charleston *Post and Courier* that "blacks and whites are mixing more these days than ever before."

Less than four months after Howard's death, however, the Laurens School District 55 Board of Trustees announced a bond referendum that would have raised $109 million for improvements to educational facilities across the county and funded the construction of a new high school. The announcement generated immediate pushback, and within weeks the vote had split along racial lines. Reverend Kennedy—a vocal proponent of the measure and outspoken supporter of the district's African American superintendent, Dr. Stephen Peters—spoke about Laurens's "racist history" and "lack of progress" at a local meeting of the NAACP. It did not go over well.

"I thought it was bull crap," Dianne Belsom, founder of the Laurens County Tea Party, later told reporters. "Instead of celebrating the gains we've made, he's just a race-baiter stuck in the past." Kennedy endured an enormous wave of criticism for his particular style of activism (which included protesting outside Belsom's home with a bullhorn). Equally as active, however, was the "Vote No" contingent. Sharon Barnes, owner of a picture frame shop on the square, offered a prize to the first person who delivered one hundred signatures of Laurens residents in opposition to the referendum—four signed prints of Confederate officers J.E.B. Stuart, Robert E. Lee, Stonewall Jackson, and Nathan Bedford Forrest.

By the time it was over—the referendum was struck down by a margin of 54 percent—many residents had called for the resignation of the entire school board. Superintendent Peters admitted that he felt unsafe in Laurens and took an abrupt leave of absence for "family reasons." As for the reverend, social media lit up with posts describing him as a "racist," a "racial pot stirrer," and a "trouble-maker" who was guilty of "preaching hate." Countless residents suggested they vote "to remove *him* from Laurens County." Just about everyone agreed that Kennedy should stop seeking attention and let the past stay in the past.

Reverend Kennedy still owns the deed to the Echo theater. He still hopes to open his long-prayed-for multicultural center, or perhaps turn the building into an auxiliary facility for his Baptist church. More recently he's floated the idea of creating a memorial for the victims of lynching—but money is tight. In the meantime, the residents of Laurens have grown used to reporters milling around, so they're a little more guarded, a little more wary. Most have tired of talking about the Redneck Shop. After all, the Echo is empty now, just another faded storefront on the courthouse square, a relic from some darker time they'd just as soon forget.

ACKNOWLEDGMENTS

Sharing the story of Michael Burden's journey to redemption and Reverend Kennedy's remarkable faith was a twenty-year passion project—but not mine. I was a freshman in high school in 1996, blissfully unaware of the Redneck Shop and the attendant controversy in Laurens. Were it not for Andrew Heckler's determination to get his film made, the book you are holding in your hands would not exist. I am profoundly grateful to Andrew for supporting another writer as she reported and interpreted a story that has been so close to him for the better part of two decades.

Some five years after Andrew wrote the first draft of his screenplay, the estimable producer Robbie Brenner signed on in the hope of shepherding *Burden* to the big screen. Fast-forward another few years, and producer Dan Farah had come on board, bringing with him truckloads of experience straddling the worlds of motion pictures and publishing. Movies are bound by a host of logistical and budgetary constraints; and filmmakers have the unenviable task of depicting a fully realized narrative in the span of roughly two hours. It was Dan who first believed that the events depicted in *Burden* could—and should—form the basis for a work of narrative nonfiction. Andrew and Robbie graciously introduced me to their contacts in Laurens, while Dan encouraged me to do what journalists do: follow the story, no matter where it might take me. What came out of my research was a tale neither simple nor tidy, but I left Laurens with an even greater appreciation for Reverend Kennedy's stunning act of grace.

My agent, Yfat Reiss Gendell, has been my professional rock and touchstone for more than five years now—thank you for pushing me out of my comfort zone. I'm so glad you're on this journey with me. My heartfelt thanks to the entire team at Foundry Literary + Media, especially Jessica Felleman.

Derek Reed, my incredible editor: you are a saint. I can't tell you how much I appreciate your thoughtful guidance, your grace under pressure, and—certainly not least—your patience. I am incredibly lucky to have been paired on this project with you. To Tina Constable, Campbell Wharton, Megan Perritt, Ayelet Gruenspecht, Cindy Berman, Maria Spano, Jessie Bright, Marlene Glazer, and the entire team at Convergent: thank you for your unwavering faith and support, even when things started to move slower than perhaps all of us had expected.

Reconstructing events that took place some twenty years ago—or, in some cases, sixty years ago—required a deep dive into the archives. A hearty thanks to the staffs at the Presbyterian College library, the Laurens County Public Library, and the Laurens Clerk of Court's office. Thom Berry and Mary C. Perry at the South Carolina State Law Enforcement Division's Freedom of Information Office swiftly fielded a number of my requests. Reverend Kennedy's former attorneys Rauch Wise and Stephen John Henry were both gracious enough to answer questions and to provide additional court records and other legal paperwork.

The process of writing a book is often a lonely one; my parents, Thomas and Cindy, were there when I needed them, as they always are—I could not have made it through without you. To Beck, for being a sounding board, a confidante, and for keeping me grounded. To Abigail Carpenter, who waited so patiently even when I was supposed to be helping plan her wedding. I owe you. (And to Laura Langdon and Deb Boudreaux, for stepping in and taking over when I was seriously short on both time and sanity—finally, we can *laissez les bons temps rouler.*) To the dear friends who somehow remained my dear friends, even as I missed birthdays and engagements, rescheduled meetings, or in some cases disappeared entirely for a matter of months, especially Christy Webster, Martinique Teperman, Kathryn Huck, Tammy Chen, and Tynan Davis.

Finally, I must express my profound gratitude to Reverend David Kennedy, Janice Kennedy, the Kennedy family, and the entire congregation at New Beginning Missionary Baptist for welcoming me into your homes and into your church. I, too, believe that you're overdue for a blessing. To Clarence and Barbara Simpson, thank you for your generosity and your insights— you both make excellent tour guides. To Judy Burden and Stacy Harbeson, I am in awe of your strength and your bravery. And to Michael Burden, for having the courage to share your story with the world.

NOTES AND SOURCES

The bulk of my reporting relies on interviews conducted with Reverend David Kennedy and members of his extended family; Reverend Clarence Simpson and his wife, Barbara; Michael and Judy Burden, and Judy's daughter, Stacy Harbeson; court records from the Laurens County courthouse; and the *Greenville News, Laurens County Advertiser*, and *Clinton Chronicle*. Reconstructing events some twenty years after the fact presents a challenge; in instances where my interview subjects have disagreed, or their memories of events have proven contradictory, I've done my best to corroborate anecdotes and dialogue with as many outside sources as possible. Additional sources for each chapter can be found below.

Prologue: "This Is What We'll Do"

Information about the history and economic development of Laurens was culled from a variety of sources, most important, the Online Records Index of the South Carolina Department of Archives and History (nationalregister.sc.gov), in particular Jennifer Revels, "Historic and Architectural Survey of Eastern Laurens County" (2003); Mary Sherrer and Jennifer Revels, "Historic and

Architectural Survey of Western Laurens County" (2002); and the National Register of Historic Places Nomination Forms prepared by John C. Blythe Jr. (1986). See also Libby Rhodes, *Images of America: Laurens* (Arcadia Publishing, 2000), and Julian Stevenson Bolick, *A Laurens County Sketchbook* (Clinton, SC: Jacobs, 1973). Information on the Capitol and Echo theaters comes from the *Laurens County Advertiser*, January 21, 1974, and is summarized at scmovietheaters .com and capitoltheaterandcafe.com. Additional sources include the Laurens County Museum, the Main Street Laurens Partnership, and Fritz Hammer's "From Cracked to Perfect Bottles: Laurens Glass Works, 1910–1986," in *Proceedings of the South Carolina Historical Association*, 2003, 25–38.

Information about the economic downturn in Laurens specifically and the decline of the textile industry in general is based on reporting from a range of government sources and trade publications, including the United States Department of Agriculture Economic Research Service. See Mark Mittelhauser, "Employment Trends in Textiles and Apparel, 1973–2005," in *Monthly Labor Review*, August 1997, 24–36; Kai Ryssdal, "In Upstate S.C., BMW Jobs Replace Textile Mills," *Marketplace*, January 17, 2014; Betty Joice Nash, "When South Carolina Met BMW," *Region Focus*, Second Quarter, 2011, 20–22; and the City of Laurens Comprehensive Plan 2015–2025, prepared by the City of Laurens Planning Commission (cityoflaurenssc.com). Population figures come from the 2010 United States Census. For crime statistics, see "Laurens Ranked Among State's Most Dangerous Cities," November 2014, at golaurens.com.

In addition to my interviews with Rev. David Kennedy, much of the material about the lynching of Richard Puckett, including the quotes from Brock Coggins and Rachel Watts, comes from Bruce E. Baker's "Under the Rope: Lynching and Memory in Laurens County, South Carolina," in *Where These Memories Grow: History, Memory, and Southern Identity*, ed. W. Fitzhugh Brundage (Chapel Hill: University of North Carolina Press, 2000), 319–346. Additional details about Puckett's death can be found in Bruce E. Baker,

This Mob Will Surely Take My Life: Lynchings in the Carolinas, 1871–1947 (Bloomsbury Academic, 2008), 121–144. See also *Greenville News*, August 12, 1913; *Laurens Advertiser*, August 13, 1913; Newberry *Herald and News*, August 13, 1913; Pickens *Keowee Courier*, August 13, 1913; *Greenwood Index* and *Greenwood Evening Index*, August 14, 1913; and *Manning Times*, August 20, 1913. The statistics about lynching in Laurens County come from the Equal Justice Initiative's "Lynching in America: Confronting the Legacy of Racial Terror" report, 3rd ed. (lynchinginamerica.eji.org/report). Samuel A. Shipman's recollections are from April 2000 interviews with G. Kurt Piehler and Shelley Stafford for the Veteran's Oral History Project, Center for the Study of War and Society, Department of History, University of Tennessee, Knoxville (vol web.utk.edu/~wpcsws/wp-content/uploads/2013/04/2000-Shipman -Samuel.pdf). Information about the trestle over River Street and its removal can be found in the *Greenville News*, September 8, 1983. Rev. Kennedy's remarks about the Ku Klux Klan growing "bold" are from the Associated Press, June 17, 1996. The Gray Court resident who preferred to keep her mind on the Bible was quoted in the *Greenville News*, March 5, 1996.

One: The Mask That Grins and Lies

Much of the narrative in this chapter derives from my interviews with Reverend Kennedy and members of his extended family. Frankie Kennedy's specific recollections of her son's death come from videotaped interviews conducted in the mid-2000s by Mary Jo Marino Stemp, to whom I am grateful.

For more general information about the Echo theater, see my notes for the Prologue. The city's plans to revitalize the courthouse square were covered in the *Greenville News*, June 27, 1983. Advertisements for the liquidation of the Echo and its contents can be found in the Greenwood *Index-Journal*, August 6 and August 13, 1989.

The statistics regarding the number of meals served by the

Laurens County Soup Kitchen come from a feature in the *Laurens County Advertiser*, October 16, 1996.

The description of Bell's Café was largely derived from interviews with Clarence Simpson. For Samuel Shipman, see my notes for the Prologue. The death of the Laurens County sharecropper was covered in the *Greenville News*, July 5, September 24, and November 16, 1957, and the Greenwood *Index-Journal*, July 10, 1957. For an account of the Lamar riots, widely regarded as the most violent reaction to court-ordered desegregation in South Carolina, see the Associated Press report in the Greenwood *Index-Journal*, August 27, 1970.

Benjamin Payton's biography was culled from obituaries printed in the *New York Times*, October 11, 2016, and the *Montgomery Advertiser*, September 30, 2016. The quote about Benedict College's original mission (to train "teachers and preachers") comes from the Benedict College Catalogue and is summarized at benedict.edu. For an account of the Lawson Affair, see Ray Waddle, "Days of Thunder," *Vanderbilt Magazine*, Fall 2002.

For an overview of the Anti–Drug Abuse Act and its effect on the national prison population, see Deborah J. Vagins and Jesselyn McCurdy, "Cracks in the System: Twenty Years of the Unjust Federal Crack Cocaine Law," American Civil Liberties Union, October 2006. For specific information on the Abbeville bust, see the *Greenville News*, April 12 and 13, 1986. For an account of the rumors about the Anderson County Sheriff, see the *Greenville News*, February 28 and March 22, 1986. For an overview of the Laurens raid, see Associated Press reports in the *Gaffney Ledger*, September 23, 1985, and Greenwood *Index-Journal*, December 4, 1985. See also the Greenwood *Index-Journal*, September 22, 1985, and *Greenville News*, October 10, 1985.

Reverend Kennedy's first major anti-drug rally in Laurens was covered in the *Greenville News*, December 23, 1986, and January 18, 1987. Mayor Dominick's visit to New Beginning and the statistics about drug arrests in Laurens are from January 16, 1987.

For information about the arrest of William Robertson, see the *Greenville News,* October 6 and October 12, 1988. Kennedy's specific quotes about turning the city "upside down" are from the *Greenville News,* October 16, 1988.

Worsening racial tensions, including a lawsuit filed by the local NAACP and a lawsuit filed by a Laurens parent against the local school board, were covered in the *Greenville News,* March 8 and April 15, 1990. Kennedy's quotes about encouraging children to boycott classes are from the *Greenville News,* August 30, 1989.

Almost all of the information about the death of James "Bobo" Cook, the resulting protests, and the fallout between Reverend Kennedy and Mayor Bob Dominick comes from coverage in the *Greenville News* in 1990: The initial protest rally was covered on April 10; the verbal altercation and Dominick's quotes about Project Awakening are from June 19; Dominick's reference to Rev. Kennedy as a "joker" and Councilman Bolt's comments are from June 20; the physical confrontation between Dominick and Kennedy was covered on June 23. For information about Kennedy's trial, see June 27, August 26, and August 29; and for city prosecutor Wyatt Saunders's comments on the "racial overtones" of the case, see the January 4, 1991, issue. The Greenwood *Index-Journal,* April 10, 1990, also reported on the Cook protests.

Two: A Kernel of Truth

The controversial death of Bobby "Cat" Scroggs triggered investigations by the FBI and the South Carolina State Law Enforcement Division, and was covered extensively in the *Greenville News.* Most of my information comes from a four-part investigative series by Jim Tharpe. John Howard's press conference and the quotes about returning to reveal "all of the facts" gleaned during the Klan's probe of the incident are from the third installment of that series, May 1, 1980.

To trace John Howard's rise through the Klan from the late

1960s to the mid-1970s (and for information on various civil-rights-
era Klansmen, in particular Robert Scoggin and James Venable),
I relied heavily on the comprehensive reporting in Patsy Sims's
The Klan, 2nd ed. (University Press of Kentucky, 1996). (In some
instances, I have altered Sims's rendering of the southern dialect,
for clarity.) Howard's quote about being "scared" by civil-rights-
era rioting is from the *Clinton Chronicle*, March 20, 1996. Howard's
thoughts about Reconstruction-era South Carolina and the formation of the Ku Klux Klan (specifically, the idea that the Klan was
formed to defend oppressed southern whites) are represented in a
range of articles and confirmed by my interviews with Michael Burden; the specific quotes about African Americans "ruling and dic-
tating" southern white people are from a YouTube video uploaded
on October 2, 2011, by Max Wendroff (youtube.com/watch?v=fJQe
SsnaPs8&t=136s). As it relates to the 1970 death of Willie Odom,
Sims reported that John Howard, Robert Scoggin, and several
other Klansmen were arrested and indicted, and that bail was set "at
five to seven thousand dollars." For additional information, see the
Washington Post, September 18, 1970, the *Greenville News*, November 10, 1971, and Associated Press reports in the *Aiken Standard*,
October 14, 1970, and the Greenwood *Index-Journal*, October 28,
1970. Anne Thomson Sheppard's letter to the editor lamenting her
fear of the Klan ("Smothering in Whispers About Fear") and John
Howard's response are both from the *Greenville News*, November 1
and November 10, 1971, respectively. The 1961 assault on future
congressman John Lewis in Rock Hill, South Carolina, has been
reported on extensively, in large part because Lewis's attacker,
Elwin Wilson, publicly apologized in 2009. For a definitive account
of the apology and the resulting reunion of Lewis and Wilson,
see the Rock Hill *Herald*, January 24, January 27, and February 4,
2009. For details about John Howard's rally in Greenwood, see the
Greenwood *Index-Journal*, August 25, 1975. For additional information about Howard's split from the National Knights, see the
Associated Press reports in the *Greenville News*, October 10, 1975,

and the Muncie *Star Press*, February 9, 1976. The Southern Poverty Law Center's civil suit against Robert Shelton and the UKA was chronicled in Laurence Leamer's *The Lynching: The Epic Courtroom Battle That Brought Down the Klan* (William Morrow, 2016). For a brief account of Venable's life and health, see his obituary in the *New York Times*, January 21, 1993. Barry Black's years-long membership in the Klan is detailed in an Extremist Profile compiled by the Southern Poverty Law Center (splcenter.org). For details of his arrest record, see the *Pittsburgh Post-Gazette*, August 9, 1998. Estimating the size of any Klan faction is a notoriously difficult task, as Klansmen are known to exaggerate, obfuscate, or outright lie about membership numbers; statistics on the Keystone Klan's size under Black come from the *Washington Post*, January 24, 1999. Based on interviews with multiple subjects, the 1999 figures are likely similar to membership levels in 1993–1994. John Howard's 1992 purchase of the Echo theater was recorded in Deed Book 273, page 260, at the Laurens County Clerk of Court's office. The Articles of Incorporation for the South Carolina chapter of the Keystone Knights can be viewed online at search.laurensdeeds.com.

The more general material about the first, second, and third iterations of the Ku Klux Klan is derived from sources far too extensive to list in their entirety. Some of the most valuable and informative include Arnold Forster and Benjamin R. Epstein, "Report on the Ku Klux Klan" (Anti-Defamation League of B'nai B'rith, 1965); Elaine Frantz Parsons, *Ku-Klux: The Birth of the Klan During Reconstruction* (University of North Carolina, 2016); David Cunningham, *Klansville, U.S.A.: The Rise and Fall of the Civil Rights–Era Ku Klux Klan* (Oxford University Press, 2012); Linda Gordon, *The Second Coming of the KKK: The Ku Klux Klan of the 1920s and the American Political Tradition* (Liveright, 2017); and "Ku Klux Klan: A History of Racism," 6th ed., 2011, compiled by the Klanwatch Project of the Southern Poverty Law Center (the description of William Joseph Simmons as a "compulsive joiner" and the information about the Alabama divorcée beaten for the "crime" of remarrying both come from this report). See also Joshua Zeitz, "When Congress Ousted a Failing President," *Politico*, May 20, 2017; Joshua Rothman, "When Bigotry Paraded Through the Streets," *The Atlantic*, December 4, 2016; Kelly J. Baker, "Make America White Again?," *The Atlantic*, March 12, 2016; and Otto H. Olsen, "The Ku Klux Klan: A Study in Reconstruction Politics and Propaganda," *North Carolina Historical Review* 39, no. 3 (July 1962): 340–362.

The Laurens Riot of 1870 has been covered in an array of articles; for an overview, see Bruce E. Baker, *This Mob Will Surely Take My Life: Lynchings in the Carolinas, 1871–1947* (Bloomsbury Academic, 2008). That only sixty-five people were imprisoned as a result of the Ku Klux Klan acts comes from Shawn Alexander, *Reconstruction Violence and the Ku Klux Klan Hearings* (Bedford/St. Martin's, 2015). For information about the release of *The Birth of a Nation* and its relevance to the formation of the second Klan, see Michael S. Rosenwald, "The Ku Klux Klan Was Dead. The First Hollywood Blockbuster Revived It," *Washington Post*, August 12, 2017, and Rian Dundon, "Why Does the Ku Klux Klan Burn Crosses? They Got the Idea from a Movie," *Timeline*, March 15, 2017. The detail about Clark and Tyler having been arrested at a house of "ill repute" is from the New York *World* exposé. The abduction and decapitation of Filmore Watt Daniel and Thomas Fletcher Richard, which became known as the Mer Rouge case, attracted national attention; for an overview, see the *New York Times*, December 27, 1922.

Though the Klan today is fractured and marginalized, the idea that it may, in fact, be more dangerous than previous incarnations was informed by John Drabble's "From White Supremacy to White Power: The FBI, COINTELPRO–WHITE HATE, and the Nazification of the Ku Klux Klan in the 1970s," *American Studies* 48, no. 3 (Fall 2007): 49–74. Information here and in later chapters on leaderless resistance is culled from Jason Burke, "The Myth of the 'Lone Wolf' Terrorist," *The Guardian*, March 30, 2017; Mike German, "Behind the Long Terrorist, a Pack Mentality," *Washington Post*, June 5, 2005; Laura Smith, "Armed Resistance, Lone Wolves,

and Media Messaging: Meet the Godfather of the 'Alt-Right,'"
Timeline, November 6, 2017; Mike Isaacson, "The Real Origins of
'Lone Wolf' White Supremacists like Dylann Roof," *ThinkProgress*,
June 24, 2015; and David Cunningham, "Five Myths About the Ku
Klux Klan," *Washington Post*, March 11, 2016.

Three: The Perfect Recruit

Much has been written about the Ku Klux Klan's moneymaking
apparatus, particularly during the Simmons era of the 1920s. For
an overview of the Klan's financial dealings and dues schedule, see
Roland G. Fryer Jr. and Steve D. Levitt, "Hatred and Profits: Under
of the Hood of the Ku Klux Klan," *Quarterly Journal of Economics* 127, no. 4 (2012): 1883–1925. Specific information about Bessie
Tyler's palatial Buckhead residence comes from the National Register of Historic Places Nomination Forms prepared by Steven Moff-
son (2005) and is summarized on the Buckhead Heritage Society
website (buckheadheritage.com). The detail about the UKA's Bob
Jones and his Cadillac is from the "Klansville U.S.A." documentary
on PBS, which is summarized on pbs.org.

Michael Burden has recounted his first meeting with John Howard and his initiation into the Klan in a variety of articles and interviews; though the basic outline of his story remains the same, the
details vary. In Eric Harrison's account for the *Los Angeles Times*,
"A Tale of Faith, Hope, and Hate," July 30, 1997, Burden says he
first met Howard in 1989—and later revises that to 1986. Harrison
also reports that Burden was sleeping in an abandoned vehicle. In
Monte Paulson's article for the Columbia *State*, "Redneck Shop in
Precarious Place," May 24, 1997, Burden was spending most nights
"in a friend's car." (Burden's quote about having "ate, slept, drank
and studied" the Klan also comes from this article.) That Burden's
biological parents were once members of the Klan is corroborated
by an August 2009 deposition of John Howard in the matter of *New
Beginning Baptist Church vs. Michael Eugene Burden, John Howard,*

Hazel Howard, and Nicholas Edward Chappell, provided to me by attorney Rauch Wise, to whom I am grateful. (Howard's decision to deed the Redneck Shop to Burden, as a matter of legal protection, is also confirmed by the deposition.)

Bill Riccio's admission to combing shopping malls and swimming pools in search of prospective recruits, as well as numerous accounts of Riccio's alleged sex abuse, are from the Southern Poverty Law Center's *Intelligence Report*, Fall 2007 issue.

The quote from the Anti-Defamation League about Robert Shelton having "no other interests" beyond the KKK comes from David Cunningham, *Klansville, U.S.A.: The Rise and Fall of the Civil Rights–Era Ku Klux Klan* (Oxford University Press, 2012), 39. John Howard's reverence for William Joseph Simmons and the 1920s-era Ku Klux Klan has been documented in a range of articles, including the *Clinton Chronicle*, March 20, 1996, and Frank Beacham, "A Visit to the Redneck Shop," *Orlando Weekly*, January 23, 1997; the specific quotes about Simmons and his "vision in the sky" are from a YouTube video uploaded on October 2, 2011, by Max Wendroff (youtube.com/watch?v=fJQeSsnaPs8&t=136s). The counterfeit photograph of black Confederate soldiers is clearly visible in a YouTube video uploaded on August 24, 2010, by skier137 (https://www.youtube.com/watch?v=F1hshzHWG0c). The provenance of the photo, however, is described in detail in Jerome S. Handler and Michael L. Tuite, Jr. "Retouching History: The Modern Falsification of a Civil War Photograph," 2007, online at http://people.virginia.edu/~jh3v/retouchinghistory/essay.html#11. For information on the origin of the MIOAK, see the Anti-Defamation League's website, https://www.adl.org/education/references/hate-symbols/blood-drop-cross. For information about cross-burning and its depiction in *The Birth of a Nation*, see my notes for Chapter Two.

An enormous amount has been written about the Greensboro Massacre of 1979. For a definitive account, see Jason Kops, "The Greensboro Massacre: A Challenge to Accepted Historical Interpretations," *Explorations* 7 (2012): 76–86, https://uncw.edu/csurf

/Explorations/documents/JasonKops.pdf. James Farrands's quotes about being a "new breed" of Klansman are from William Sherman, "The Boys in the Hoods," *Mirabella*, September 1992. His eventual banishment of neo-Nazis from the Invisible Empire is described in the *Asheville Times-Citizen*, June 20, 1993. The statistic about John Howard's Klan faction having but forty members is from the Orangeburg *Times and Democrat*, January 1, 1981. The resurgence of the Klan in South Carolina, Charles Murphy's quotes about the "new and better leadership" of Horace King, and the SLED chief's belief that people were "too smart" to join the Klan are from the *Greenville News*, August 29, 1985. For information about the marches in Clinton and Laurens (and the relevant lawsuits filed by the Klan), see the *Greenville News*, October 24, 1985.

The information about Shelton's arrival at the Indian Springs meeting is culled from reporting in Patsy Sims's *The Klan*, 2nd ed. (University Press of Kentucky, 1996) and from Cunningham's *Klansville, U.S.A.* The specific information about Michael Burden's weapons cache and acquired books on explosives comes from South Carolina State Law Enforcement Division (SLED) Notes pertaining to case number P97-260, obtained via Freedom of Information Act request.

The account of William "Wild Bill" Hoff's childhood in south Brooklyn, his discharge from the Navy, and his subsequent descent into the world of organized hate largely comes from reporting in the Elmira *Star-Gazette*, August 28, 1969, and from interviews his brother Sheldon granted with the Southern Poverty Law Center's *Intelligence Report*, Fall 2007 issue. See also *New York Times*, October 12, 1968, and August 14, 1969, and the Elmira *Star-Gazette*, April 20, 2007. Details of Hoff's employment at and dismissal from the Third World Employment Agency can be found in an Associated Press report in the Phoenix *Arizona Republic*, May 24, 1992. Hoff's "tall tales" of his time as a mercenary and his former run for Senate are summarized in several of the above articles, as well as in Robert Dalton, "A Force in NSM Carried Secret to His Grave," goupstate.com, April 15, 2007. A number of posts on the Vanguard News Network forum, a white supremacist website, further propagate rumors of Hoff's life within the movement. See especially vnnforum.com/showthread.php?t=41685 and vnnforum.com/show thread.php?t=24876.

Jack Levin's quotes about Burden being a "perfect recruit" are from Paulson, "Redneck Shop in Precarious Place." Kathlee Blee's quotes are from Mike Sajna, "Pitt Researcher Dispels Many Myths About KKK's Members," *University Times* 29, no. 5 (April 1997) (www.utimes.pitt.edu/archives/?p=5301).

For information about the collapse of the Riegel mill in Ware Shoals, see the UPI archives, August 13, 1982 (https://www.upi.com /Archives/1982/08/13/The-Riegel-Textile-Corp-has-announced -that-850-millworkers/5590398059200) and the *New York Times*, December 22, 1984. The statistic about the closing of thirty South Carolina manufacturing plants in 1983 alone is from the *Greenville News*, March 8, 1994. The information about the restaurant proprietor in Iva is from the *Greenville News*, December 13, 1995. The quote about the collapse of the Milliken mill potentially being a "death bell" comes from an Associated Press report in the Greenwood *Index-Journal*, July 27, 1994. For information about the decline of business in the Laurens courthouse square, see the *Greenville News*, September 5, 1985.

The auction of Klan memorabilia in Freemont, Michigan, that fetched nearly $30,000 was covered in the *Greenville News*, November 1, 1992.

Michael Burden's remainder interest in John Howard's life estate ownership of the Echo theater was recorded in Deed Book 315, page 55, at the Laurens County Clerk of Court's office. Barry Black's ninety-nine-year lease on the Echo can be viewed online at search.laurensdeeds.com.

Four: Burn It Down

Reverend Kennedy's preemptive attempts to shut down the Redneck Shop are described in Monte Paulson, "Redneck Shop in Precarious Place," Columbia *State*, May 24, 1997. For statistics on the representation of the African American community in Laurens (and for Marian Miller's quote about Project Awakening), see the *Greenville News*, April 15, 1990. For information on the Ware Shoals church experiencing intimidation by members of the Klan, see the Greenwood *Index-Journal*, August 14, 1994. For the closure of Lydia Mill and Laurens Glass, see the *Laurens County Advertiser*, March 27 and April 10, 1996, and the Clinton *Chronicle*, March 27, 1996.

Ed McDaniel's appearance before the County Council was reported in the *Laurens County Advertiser*, March 13, 1996, and the *Clinton Chronicle*, March 13, 1996. For information on his unity ribbon campaign, see the *Laurens County Advertiser*, March 15, 1996. The information from *Site Selection* magazine comes from the *Greenville News*, December 10, 1998. For additional information about the Redneck Shop's grand opening, see the *Greenville News*, March 5 and March 8, 1996, and the *Washington Post*, May 30, 1996. John Howard's quote about his desire for respect from the African American community, as well as Sheriff Robin Morse's quote about having "no beef" with Howard, are both from the *Laurens County Advertiser*, March 6, 1996. The Channel 7 News piece is available in full on YouTube, uploaded to the site on October 29, 2010, by jabbertube (youtube.com/watch?v=cJYiouB83is). The "Your Two Cents" column appeared in the *Laurens County Advertiser*, March 15, 1996. The anecdote about the "codger" who threatened a black customer is from Mike Pulley, "Shopping with the Klan," *Sacramento News and Review*, September 12, 1996. John Howard's claim that he knew "just how a black person felt" is from an Associated Press report in the Greenwood *Index-Journal*, March 14, 1996.

The meeting at Rev. Kennedy's church, during which Councilwoman Miller warned demonstrators to be cautious and careful, was covered by the *Greenville News*, March 11, 1996. For Rev. Kennedy's first protest rally against the Redneck Shop, as well as Rev. Jesse Jackson's arrival in Laurens, see the *Laurens County Advertiser*, March 20 and March 22, 1996; the *Clinton Chronicle*, March 20, 1996; and the Associated Press report in the *Greenwood Index-Journal*, March 17, 1996. The near-arrest of a local Klansman was covered in the *Greenville News*, March 17, 1996. For David Prichard Hunter's vandalism, see the *Laurens County Advertiser*, March 27, 1996, the Associated Press report in the *Gaffney Ledger*, March 25, 1996, the *Greenville News*, March 26, 1996, and the *Clinton Chronicle*, March 27, 1996.

Five: *Non Silba Sed Anthar*

Howard's damages claim and the quotes from David Prichard Hunter's defense attorney are from the *Greenville News*, April 5 and May 8, 1996. For information on the Janet Reno–led investigation, see the *Greenville News*, March 21, 1996. The detail about John Howard's bank asking him to close his account is from an Associated Press report in the Orangeburg *Times and Democrat*, March 19, 1996.

The Laurens County Council's approval of Ed McDaniel's proposed anti-Klan resolution was covered in the *Laurens County Advertiser*, March 27, 1996, and the *Clinton Chronicle*, March 27, 1996. The quote from Jim Coleman comes from McDaniel's obituary, March 18, 2015, at golaurens.com. For information about Councilman McDaniel's Unity Forum, see the *Laurens County Advertiser*, April 5, 1996, and the *Clinton Chronicle*, April 10 and April 12, 1996.

For Reverend Kennedy's appearance before South Carolina's legislative Black Caucus, as well as the Caucus's response to the Redneck Shop and general tensions with Governor Beasley, see: the *Greenville News*, March 15, April 25, and September 2, 1995, and January 6, 1996, and Associated Press reports in the Greenwood *Index-Journal*, June 14 and December 20, 1995. For worsening race relations in South Carolina, see the *Greenville News*, April 14 and May 3, 1996; the Associated Press report in the Orangeburg *Times and Democrat*, May 3, 1996; the Associated Press report in the Greenwood *Index-Journal*, March 20, 1996; and the *Baltimore Sun*, June 30, 1996. Rev. Kennedy's warning about an imminent race war comes from an Associated Press report in the Greenwood *Index-Journal*, April 25, 1996.

For a more general account of Martin Luther King Jr.'s commitment to nonviolent resistance and his legacy, see Mark Engler and Paul Engler, "MLK Was a Disruptor," *Salon*, January 18, 2016, and Matt Berman, "The Forgotten Martin Luther King: A Radical Anti-War Leftist," *The Atlantic*, March 28, 2013. For a full transcript of King's remarks before the Rabbinical Assembly on March 25, 1968, see rabbinicalassembly.org. Rev. Jesse Jackson's reference to King as a "civil rights teddy bear" is from Drew Dellinger, "The Ecological King: A Vision for Our Times," Institute of Noetic Sciences, January 16, 2017.

The career history of attorney Suzanne Coe was culled from a variety of articles, in particular the *Greenville News*, August 15, 1993; the Columbia *State*, July 21, 1996; and an Associated Press report in the *Pensacola News Journal*, June 3, 1995. For more information about Coe's representation of local gentlemen's club Diamonds, see the *Greenville News*, December 1, 1994, June 15, July 19, and October 6, 1995. Coe's quote about not wanting to take John Howard's case is from the *New York Times*, November 17, 1996. The detail about the words "Jesus Loves Everybody" being painted on the door of the Redneck Shop comes from the *Greenville News*, April 12, 1996.

For an overview of the Sons of Confederate Veterans, see the Southern Poverty Law Center's *Intelligence Report*, Summer 2000 and Spring 2002 issues. See also Jon Elliston, "Between Heritage and Hate," *Ashville Mountain Xpress*, August 18, 2004, and Katy Waldman, "Guardians of White Innocence," *Slate*, September 25, 2017. For information about Linda Sewell, see the Southern Poverty

Law Center's *Intelligence Report,* Spring 2003. The *Larry King Live* interview is available on YouTube, uploaded May 22, 2011, by user Daniel Martin (youtube.com/watch?v=PZmBvHMev4g).

For information about the Klan "hotline," see the *Washington Post,* May 30, 1996.

Barry Black's promise to leave Laurens for "a million dollars" comes from an Associated Press report in the Greenwood *Index-Journal,* March 17, 1996. Black's boast about having acquired a print of the Puckett lynching appeared in Harry Allen, "Shop of Horrors," *Vibe,* June–July 1996. Evidence of the Redneck Shop's sale of the Puckett photo appears in Bruce E. Baker's "Under the Rope: Lynching and Memory in Laurens County, South Carolina," in *Where These Memories Grow: History, Memory, and Southern Identity,* ed. W. Fitzhugh Brundage (Chapel Hill: University of North Carolina Press, 2000), 319–346. See also the Greenwood *Index-Journal,* May 13, 1996. The quotes from Teddy Craine, Roger Stowe, and Stephanie Wilke are from the *Greenville News,* July 20, 1996; the *Washington Post,* May 30, 1996; and the *Washington Post,* March 18, 1996, respectively.

Reverend Kennedy's second rally against the Redneck Shop was reported in the *Greenville News,* April 17 and April 28, 1996, and the *Clinton Chronicle,* April 24, 1996.

Michael Burden has described the near assassination of Reverend Kennedy in a variety of articles, including Monte Paulson, "Redneck Shop in Precarious Place," Columbia *State,* May 24, 1997, and Eric Harrison, "A Tale of Faith, Hope, and Hate," *Los Angeles Times,* July 30, 1997. The precise date of the altercation, however, is difficult to determine. Paulson reports that it occurred sometime in February 1996, weeks before the shop opened. Based on interviews with Burden and Rev. Kennedy, I believe the altercation most likely took place in April.

Six: "Choose"

For John Howard's defamation lawsuit against Councilman Ed McDaniel, see Laurens County court record 96-CP30-228. Details of the suit can also be found in the *Clinton Chronicle*, May 15 and June 12, 1996, and the *Laurens County Advertiser*, May 8, 1996. Howard's quote about Rev. Kennedy getting "in trouble" is from the *Clinton Chronicle*, May 1, 1996.

For details about the arrest of Herbert Neely and William Hoff, see the *Clinton Chronicle*, May 29 and July 17, 1996, and the *Laurens County Advertiser*, May 22, 1996.

Horace King's involvement in the fires at Macedonia Baptist and Mount Zion AME has been written about extensively. For a definitive account, see Sandra E. Johnson, *Standing on Holy Ground: A Triumph over Hate Crime in the Deep South* (St. Martin's Press, 2002) and Michael Chandler's documentary film *Forgotten Fires*, Pack Creed Productions, 1998. For a general overview of the 1996 church fires across the south, see Martin Walker, "Fire and Loathing," *The Guardian*, July 13, 1996. King's quote about his childhood comes from the Orangeburg *Times and Democrat*, July 1997 (reprinted online at thetandd.com on July 20, 2008). The rally at his home in Pelion was covered by Susan Hogan-Albach and Douglas Pardue of the Knight-Ridder/Tribune news service (see *Montgomery Advertiser*, July 27, 1996). See also the Associated Press report in the Greenwood *Index-Journal*, July 1, 1996, and the *Los Angeles Times*, November 10, 1998.

The appearance of *The Bible Answers Racial Questions* at the Pelion rally was covered in the above *Montgomery Advertiser* article, as well as in an Associated Press report in the *Greenville News*, July 1, 1996. Eugene S. Hall's involvement in the Montgomery bombings was covered extensively by the *Montgomery Advertiser* in February 1957. For an account of the mock hanging in the Montgomery courthouse square, see the *Montgomery Advertiser*, August 5 and August 6, 1956. For information about the booklet's appearance in Boston, see the W. Arthur Garrity Jr. chambers papers on the Boston Schools Desegregation Case, 1972–1997, in the digital collection of the University Archives and Special Collections at UMass Boston (http://openarchives.umb.edu/cdm/landingpage/collection /p15774coll33), and the Stark and Subtle Divisions website, curated by graduate students in the History and American Studies department at UMass Boston (http://bodesca.omeka.net). The booklet's arrival at the Redneck Shop is described in the Greenwood *Index-Journal*, May 13, 1996.

Seven: "This New Beginning, Ain't It?"

Information about Rev. Kennedy's plans to construct a multicultural center in Laurens is from the *Greenville News*, July 14, 1996.

In addition to my interviews with Rev. Kennedy and Michael Burden, the account of Burden's repudiation of the Klan, his eviction from the Redneck Shop, and his subsequent apology to members of New Beginning Missionary Baptist was culled from a range of articles, including the *Greenville News*, July 10 and July 11, 1996; the *Clinton Chronicle*, July 10, 1996; and the *Laurens County Advertiser*, July 10 and July 12, 1996.

The information about homes in Laurens County in 1940 is from Jennifer Revels, "Historic and Architectural Survey of Eastern Laurens County," 2003, South Carolina Department of Archives and History (nationalregister.sc.gov).

The statistics about the unemployment rate in Laurens are from the Greenwood *Index-Journal*, December 27, 1996.

For information about Laurens city officials' plan to preemptively deny John Howard a business license, see the *Clinton Chronicle*, July 17, 1996; the *Greenville News*, July 12 and July 17, 1996; the *Laurens County Advertiser*, July 17, 1996; and the Associated Press report in the *Montgomery Advertiser*, July 21, 1996.

The quotes from Rev. Kennedy's sister, Pam, are from videotaped interviews conducted in the mid-2000s by Mary Jo Marino Stemp.

Eight: "Let's Talk Business"

For details of John Howard's lawsuit filed against the city of Laurens, see the *Greenville News*, July 20, November 7, and November 21, 1996; the *Laurens County Advertiser*, July 24, August 7, November 20, and November 22, 1996; and the *Clinton Chronicle*, July 24 and November 27, 1996. For additional details of the Laurens City Council meeting in November 1997, see the Associated Press online archives, story number w051637, November 21, 1996.

Kennedy's request for "full and public" investigations of the Redneck Shop comes from the *Laurens County Advertiser*, December 18, 1996.

Information about the SLED investigation into John Howard, as well as Michael Burden's polygraph examination, was culled from South Carolina State Law Enforcement Notes pertaining to case number P97-260, obtained via Freedom of Information Act request. The quote from Kennedy's lawyer about trusting his client's instincts toward Burden "to some degree" is from the *Los Angeles Times*, July 30, 1997. The County Council's debate over the Confederate flag at the Capitol dome was covered by the *Laurens County Advertiser*, December 11, 1996, and January 15, 1997, and the *Clinton Chronicle*, January 15, 1997. The information about the Klan's plan to open a recruiting office above the Redneck Shop is from the *Greenville News*, March 2, 1997. The account of the Redneck Shop sticker placed on the door of Rev. Kennedy's church is culled from the *Clinton Chronicle*, April 2, 1997, and the *Greenville News*, March 31 and April 1, 1997.

In addition to my interviews with Michael Burden, the account of his decision to sell the remainder interest in the Redneck Shop to Rev. Kennedy was culled from reporting in the *Laurens County Advertiser*, June 6, 1997; the *Washington Post*, July 27, 1997; and "Hope and Hate," *Primetime Live*, ABC News, ed. Jim Sabat, October 1, 1997.

Details of Dwayne Howard's arrest can be found in the *Greenville News*, May 20, May 21, June 14, and June 15, 1997; the *Laurens*

County Advertiser, May 21, 1997; and the *Clinton Chronicle*, May 21, 1997. Details of Kennedy's protests in and around Laurens throughout the fall of 1997 and the spring of 1998, including his protests of the Kemet Corp. plant closure and the Laurens County Sheriff's Department, were culled from the *Greenville News*, August 29, 1997, and February 14, 1998; and the *Clinton Chronicle*, September 3 and December 24, 1997. The October 1997 Klan rally, at which Councilman McDaniel attempted to debate demonstrators "on any subject," was covered by the *Clinton Chronicle*, October 29, 1997.

For Michael Burden's arrest record and sentencing details, see Laurens County criminal court records F822419, second-degree burglary, grand larceny; F822421, second-degree burglary; F822423, second-degree burglary, grand larceny; F822424, second-degree burglary; F909070, second-degree burglary, grand larceny; F909077, second-degree burglary, grand larceny; and F909079, second-degree burglary, grand larceny, safe-cracking. Burden's initial arrest in Woodruff was reported by GoUpstate.com on July 1, 1998 (http://www.goupstate.com/article/NC/19980701/news/605183990/SJ). Additional details about subsequent arrests can be found in the *Clinton Chronicle*, August 12 and August 26, 1998. For Investigator Chuck Milam's quotes see the *Greenville News*, August 15, 1998.

Nine: The Substance of Things Hoped for, the Evidence of Things Not Seen

For information about the four Keystone Knights arrested at a rally in Boswell, see the Allentown *Morning Call*, July 31, 1998. Barry Black's Supreme Court case battle has been reported on extensively in a wide variety of sources. For an overview of the case, see William Mears, "U.S. Supreme Court to Hear Cross Burning Arguments," CNN, December 13, 2002. For information about Horace King's trial and the collapse of the Christian Knights, see my notes for Chapter Six. Morris Dees's quote about the Christian Knights and their "day of reckoning" is from the *Montgomery Advertiser*, July 28, 1998. Bill Moore's quote about hate groups becoming more cautious in the wake of the verdict is from an Associated Press report in the Orangeburg *Times and Democrat*, July 26, 1998.

For information about the formation of the Carolina Knights and the rally in Burnettown, see the *Augusta Chronicle*, June 15 and September 17, 2000. Information about the rising number of hate groups in the early 2000s is culled from the Southern Poverty Law Center's *Intelligence Report*, Spring 2008, and Brad Knickerbocker, "Anti-Immigrant Sentiments Fuel Ku Klux Klan Resurgence," *Christian Science Monitor*, February 9, 2007. For the bar patron who believed that residents of Laurens were "past" slavery, see John Saward, "Keeping It Casual: A Day with South Carolina's 21st Century Racists," *Vice*, February 22, 2016. Information about various white supremacist events hosted by the Redneck Shop was culled from posts on a range of white supremacist websites, including Stormfront.com and WhiteReference.com, as well as reporting by the Southern Poverty Law Center and Anti-Defamation League. For the 2006 Aryan Nations "World Congress," hosted at the Redneck Shop, see John F. Sugg, "Inside the Secret World of White Supremacy," *Creative Loafing*, October 18, 2006.

Information about John Taylor Bowles and his campaign platform comes from a report in the *Columbia City Paper*, February 2007, and Wikinews interviews, February 19, 2008 (https://en.wikinews .org/wiki/Wikinews_interviews_John_Taylor_Bowles,_National _Socialist_Order_of_America_candidate_for_US_President).

For general information about the history and rise of the National Socialist Movement, see the Southern Poverty Law Center's *Intelligence Report*, Spring 2006; Sonia Scherr, "Neo-Nazi Group's Dirty Linen Aired in Leaked Emails," Southern Poverty Law Center, August 28, 2009; and "American Stormtroopers: Inside the National Socialist Movement," Anti-Defamation League Center on Extremism, 2008. For the 2007 NSM rally at the South Carolina statehouse, see the *Greenville News*, April 27, 2007, and the Associated Press report in the *Aiken Standard*, April 15, 2007. The detail about the Keystone Knights barring fraternization with neo-Nazis is from a letter to the editor published in the *Alexandria Times-*

Tribune, January 6, 1999, written by Allen Wood, Grand Klaliff of the International Keystone Knights, Realm of Indiana.

The fraudulent deeds between John Howard, Michael Burden, and Nicholas Chappell are recorded in Deed Book 809, page 226, and Deed Book 827, page 188, at the Laurens County Clerk of Court's Office, and can be viewed at search.laurensdeeds.com. Rev. Kennedy's quote about Burden "falling prey" to the Klan is from the *New York Times*, January 12, 2012.

For information about William Hoff's death and Howard's You-Tube comments, and for John Howard and Michael Burden's 2009 depositions, see my notes for Chapter Three. Nicholas Chappell's comments about Kennedy's claim to the Echo are from the *Canadian National Post*, March 24, 2008.

For Judge Frank R. Addy Jr.'s ruling in the matter of *New Beginning Baptist Church vs. Michael Eugene Burden, John Howard, Hazel Howard, and Nicholas Edward Chappell*, see Laurens County court record 2008CP3000708. See also the *Laurens County Advertiser Extra*, January 7, 2012; the *Laurens County Advertiser*, January 11, 2012; the *Greenville News*, September 2, 2008, and the Associated Press report in the *Newport News Daily Press*, March 11, 2008.

The online chatter about Rev. Kennedy's lawsuit was culled from posts at (now defunct) WhiteReference.com. For an account of the fire at Rev. Kennedy's church, see golaurens.com, September 11, 2013.

Afterword

The warning to residents of Jackson, Georgia, in advance of *Burden*'s filming was included in the "Press Release on 'Burden' by the City of Jackson," published at jacksonbuttscounty.com.

Numerous reporters have likened Donald Trump's rhetoric on the campaign trail to language employed by the 1920s-era Ku Klux Klan; see especially Kelly J. Baker, "Make America White Again?," *The Atlantic*, March 12, 2016, and Yoni Appelbaum, "Why Won't

Donald Trump Repudiate the Ku Klux Klan?," *The Atlantic*, February 28, 2016. For information about the nearly nine hundred hate incidents that took place in the ten days following the 2016 presidential election, see "Ten Days After: Harassment and Intimidation in the Aftermath of the Election," authored by Cassie Miller and Alexandra Werner-Winslow of the Southern Poverty Law Center.

John Howard's obituary can be found at the Parker-White-Pruitt Funeral Homes and Crematory's website (parkerwhitepruitt .com). Debbie Campbell's quote about blacks and whites in Laurens "mixing more these days than ever before," as well as Dianne Belsom's assertion that Reverend Kennedy is a race-baiter and Superintendent Dr. Stephen Peters's admission of feeling unsafe in Laurens, are from Adam Parker, "The Redneck Shop and the Preacher: In Laurens, A Long Saga of Racial Conflict Continues," Charleston *Post and Courier*, October 1, 2017. For information about the Laurens School District 55 Board of Trustee's proposed bond referendum, as well as the resulting racial strife, see the *Laurens County Advertiser*, August 30, September 6, September 27, and October 18, 2017.

ABOUT THE AUTHOR

COURTNEY HARGRAVE is a journalist and coauthor who has worked on numerous *New York Times* bestsellers. She lives in New York City.